BAIRAG

THE TASTE OF RENUNCIATION

BAIRAG

THE TASTE OF RENUNCIATION

By C.S.Bairagi
Charanjit Singh Bairagi

ISBN : 9788193160534
Moksh Publications

"The patterns that cannot be seen by the naked eye or understood by the thinking mind are disclosed to the single eyed witness."

CONTENTS

ACKNOWLEDGMENTS

I am deeply thankful to all the visible and invisible hands that have gone into the making of this book. Without their assistance and blessings I could not have done it. From the ones who inspired me to write to the one who has handed it to you, they all play a significant role in the manifestation of this work and have made it possible for me to reach out to you and share my being with you.

I am as grateful to those who have printed and distributed my work as I am to those who have earned for all of us the right to freedom of expression. There were days when it was not possible for an individual to speak the truth and share it with others. We are all very fortunate to be able to do so and should respect this freedom by not saying anything or writing anything that invades the space of others and hurts their sentiments. I therefore thank those who reviewed my work and provided me with a healthy feedback.

Even the tree, the wood of which the paper of this book is made from, deserves my thank you. We are all connected in a way that goes far beyond that which is obvious and we often fail to extend our gratitude to the silent existence that helps us realize our dreams. I thank everyone and everything responsible for all that I am and this book is a gift from me to mother-nature.

Charanjit Singh

CHAPTER 1 - THE WORLD OF CONSUMPTIONS

The life of an ordinary man is a life of consumptions. From something as tangible as a heavy meal, to something as subtle as an orgasm, it is nothing but a hunger and a gratification; a desire and a consumption. During most of the day, if he is not eating or drinking something then he is reading, watching or listening to something and thus feeding his senses on subtle diets. He is always consuming something or the other and when he is tired of all these consumptions, he finally shuts off everything and settles down to consume sleep. The momentum of the day frequently expresses itself in the form of dreams and the subconscious creates new ways of feeding the senses.

More than 90% of the human beings have cultivated a lifestyle that is based upon the gratification of the various hungers. They cannot even contemplate a life beyond sensual pleasures. For them, such a life is analogous to death and absolutely dull as well as tasteless. They can imagine the lack or loss of senses when they look at the deaf, dumb, blind, paralyzed and sick but the conquering of these senses by an ascetic is beyond their comprehension. They think of an ascetic as someone who is willfully depriving himself of the flavors of life and starving his body, mind and soul, thereby converting his surroundings into a graveyard. They fail to see that he is simply feeding on diets more subtle than theirs, consuming for a different purpose and from a different dimension.

We don't eat with the mouth only. We eat with our eyes, we eat with our ears, we eat with our nostrils and we eat with our finger tips. If all these entrances to our soul are shut down, we can still eat with the mind. The market place doesn't go into the details of all this; it simply reduces the whole situation to one word – desire. As long as you have got a desire for something that can be bought with money, you are a potential customer. An enlightened being may be valuable for mankind but he is not valuable for the market, though there are people smart enough to convert one into a commodity and then sell him like any other product. But that is not where he belongs. He belongs to the temple, the Ashram.

The moment we step into the market we feel like eating this, drinking that, buying this, watching that, trying this, trying that; the consumer in us goes out of control. We are coaxed into desiring, buying and consuming and it is quite natural because we live in a world of consumptions. Consumption keeps the world going and there is nothing wrong in it as long as it does not become the sole purpose of our life. The purpose of our life is not to eat, drink, sleep and indulge in all kinds of sensual pleasures; it is to wake up to the universal truth, get to know this existence and develop a communion with our source. But it gets lost in the noise of desires and temptations. Days, months, years and decades go by, without us realizing the impermanent nature of things most dear to us. We only consider the thickness of our pleasures; we don't consider their life span.

We tend to over eat everything and our natural inclination is towards indulgence. Once we have discovered a pleasure, we would like to have as much of it as we can and as often as we can. We cling to a pleasure the way a baby clings to its mother's breast and the only thing that can check our indulgence is the limitations of our body, mind and senses. Moderation and self control don't come to us as naturally as extreme and indulgence. We are born with all the hungers while fulfillment is something we have to seek and cultivate. Almost every mind needs to be tamed and disciplined. Almost every soul needs to be sculptured. The birth of an enlightened baby is an exception to the rule.

It is that first trip of alcohol, nicotine, ecstasy, L.S.D. cocaine or heroin that gets us hooked to the experience of a pleasure which is missing in our routine life and we get hooked because of the clinging nature of our mind. The discovery of a pleasure is just the first step on the path of consuming it and incorporating it into our desire system; our list of consumptions. Once we have had something that takes away our pain for some time, we have to have it on a regular basis. The pattern of addiction is absolutely simple to understand for the one who is looking at it from a distance. But for the one whose mind has been hijacked and whose soul has been captured, it is a prison with invisible bars. Whether we stuff the body with foods and drinks or the mind with chemicals that alter our consciousness or our senses with external stimuli, we are basically encouraging the consumer in us.

For the kind of consciousness most of us are born with, there is an unbearable amount of pain and suffering inherent in the paradoxes of life. We are incapable of perceiving life as a dance and can only see it as a storehouse of battles and challenges. Anything that can relieve our pain, for a few minutes or hours, fascinates us and by the time we have tried it a few times, it has already become a habit. All our consumptions are nothing but pain killers. From a cup of tea to a dose of heroine, it's all an effort to make the unbearable bearable. The greater is someone's pain, the stronger are his consumptions. At the root of every strong addiction, you will find an excruciating pain. We consume either to forget or to escape because there is something that we are unable to accommodate in our normal self. Each and every one of us has got a threshold of endurance and when things start pushing us to the edge, we have got only two options to chose from - expansion or consumption. Most of us go for consumption.

Now, genuine expansion can only come from the stretching of our comfort zone and stepping out of useless habits. But with our consumptions, we can stay where we are, and enjoy a ride through other realms of consciousness. The convincing power of things like sex, alcohol, L.S.D. ecstasy and heroine comes from their ability to transport us to a blissful dimension for a few moments. The helplessness is in our not being able to stay there. What we need to do is - wake up to the potential and limitation of each and every pleasure. Not only that, we have also to realize the price we pay for our trips to heaven in terms of health, loss of spiritual strength, professional stagnation and the corrosion of relationships. Unless and until we dare to look at the equation of pain and pleasure in our life from a wise distance, we cannot liberate our soul from the control that consumptions exercise over it.

Indulgence is not the cure for human suffering; the cure is - understanding. It is wisdom that truly relieves our pain. Most of us fail to see that the very thing we are using to relieve our pain is destined to create more of it in the future. You can take alcohol to forget your worries but after sometime alcohol itself is going to become your concern. Our suffering is a spiritual problem and the solution also has to spiritual. It cannot be chemical. It cannot come from the outside; it has to come from within. Our consumptions are basically distractions that keep us beating around the bush. If we could just meditate for the number of hours we watch our television or sit in front of a laptop, browsing unnecessary sites, we could create a better world. If we could digest the basic pains of our incarnation instead of trying to forget them, we could succeed in creating the morphine for all our agonies - the morphine of self-realization.

The extensive use of opium and its derivatives, during the last few centuries by men and women from all classes of the society, in various countries, clearly goes to prove one thing that most of us are not sufficiently prepared for the challenges of life. It also indicates that there is a fundamental error in our approach to suffering. The intensity of narcotics has been increasing through our history and the use is becoming all the more extensive. Afghanistan alone has got more than one million drug addicts to take care of. A major portion of mankind has been captured and conquered by the consumption of powerful chemical substances that have thrown their brains out of balance and robbed them of their power to decide. The wide use of syringes, for accelerating the speed at which the addiction reaches the brain through the blood stream, shows how desperate our fellow beings are, in escaping from this plane of reality.

The invention of things like alcohol, opium, morphine, heroin and cocaine was not an accident; it was nature's response to our silent screams. But if we start taking a medicine as staple food, then it is our fault. The existence rescued us from an impossible situation by showing us a possibility and introducing us to new dimensions of reality but we got the wrong message. The same L.S.D. that is killing people assisted Dr. Richard Alpert in becoming Baba Ram Dass because he interpreted it right. Opiates were used as an anesthesia while carrying out surgical operations that would have been a torture without them. Everything in this existence has its own part to play. So do all our consumptions. Even if we are enlightened, we cannot live on air and sunlight. We have to use things; we have to consume things. It is only when we are overpowered by our intakes that the equilibrium of life shifts towards degeneration and degradation.

Have you ever wondered how much more we consume than is actually required? Take sugar for example. Any dietitian will tell you that we can easily do without most of it that is there in our diet. Yet we add it to almost everything that we eat or drink. Why? Because we are addicted to it. We eat it for pleasure. If you look closely into your daily consumptions, you will find that 50% or even more of them are just for the sake of pleasure. We are always trying to derive it from this or that. We are always busy seeking it and as soon as we find it in an object, substance, person or experience, we get hooked to the thing. This is how we cultivate habits. This is how we develop addictions.

One of the feel good hormones produced by our brain is Dopamine and we get a rush of it in response to pleasurable activities like food or sex. Caffeine, nicotine, opium and all the opium derivatives increase the production of dopamine but also disrupt the way our body produces it naturally and thus throw our brain chemistry out of balance. So anyone who is not aware of the way our brain is handicapped by our chemical intakes is liable to become dependent upon them for his basic celebration of life. If we could learn how to appreciate the blue sky, the green trees, the chirping birds, the innocence of a child and all that we have got, to experience the mystery of life, we would not require things like caffeine and nicotine to be in tune with the festivity of existence. But because we have not been educated to understand and appreciate the miracles that are performed by the existence every day, we develop a habit of synthesizing happiness with our chemical consumptions.

Most of us don't consume intelligently. We go on stuffing our soul with whatever comes our way. We read anything from the newspaper, watch anything on the television, eat anything from the market and think any kind of a thought. There is very little discrimination in our choice of visible and invisible foods. Since what we are, physically, mentally, emotionally and spiritually, is a sum total of our tangible and subtle diets, we ultimately become a victim of unintelligent choices. The ideal use of our mind is in making wise decisions and consuming only that which is in harmony with the purpose of our incarnation. We should not open our mouth to everything that is edible and our senses to all that can be perceived. A filtering of all that is available to us has to be there so that only the things which are good for the health of our being reach it.

In a world where malls and markets are super loaded with thousands and thousands of unhealthy foods and drinks, anyone who does not practice self control cannot make the best of his incarnation. Food is an area where our spirituality needs to be practiced the most. If we are not disciplined here, we cannot be disciplined anywhere else. For most of us it could be the ideal point to start from. The results are visible within a month and the control gained can then be expanded into other parts of our consciousness. Our eating habits reflect upon our spiritual strength. The food we eat not only gets converted into flesh, bones and blood, it ultimately gets converted into thought. Our subtle body depends upon our solid consumptions in a very big way. The thoughts you produce after a glass of cold milk are not the same as the ones generated by a cup of strong coffee or a glass of hard liquor.

Through what we breathe, eat, drink, read, watch, listen to and touch, we connect with the rest of the existence and the thoughts produced after processing whatever we have consumed are the essence of our relationship with the cosmos. If we want this relationship to be healthy, we have to make sure that nothing unhealthy is entertained by our body, mind and senses. We can process life in such a way that it deteriorates us on all levels i.e. physical, mental, emotional and spiritual. We can also process it in a way that we evolve, grow, mature and prosper in all aspects. It all depends upon the choices we make every day and the wisdom we tap while making them. The enlightened beings also buy from the same market as all of us do and consume from the same existence, but they choose with great care and cannot be sold something they don't want to buy. They do not forget their purpose and have great respect for the preciousness of their incarnation. We often fail to listen to our silent intuition and are forced to consume things by the noise of social customs and advertising agencies. If you don't have a television set in your house you would be considered awkward by everyone but the truth is that it is one of those things which contribute to your ill health. Similarly white sugar and caffeine are also being over consumed by more than 90% of us. They should not have been embraced by domesticity the way they have been. I firmly believe that most of us need to reconsider our lifestyle and make a few intelligent changes in it.

Why do you think we consume so much? Why are we busy feeding our body, mind and senses all the time? Because that is the only way we feel alive. Our existence as something that is neither the body nor the mind or the senses is unknown to us. By consuming, we remind ourselves that "We are" or "I am". For us, the flavor of our pleasures is the flavor of life. And the truth is that to a great extent, it is. Diving into the depth of sensations can be a great way of establishing communion with life, a communion that most of us lose in our upbringing and education. A "Yes" to pleasures is a "Yes" to life. But that does not imply a "No" to pain. If life is pleasure then life is also pain. We cannot turn our back on pain and assume ourselves to be life affirmative. Pain is also one of the flavors of life. Pleasure can make you lively but it is pain that makes you wise. So, when you say "Yes" to suffering, accept it and embrace it, your consumptions drop significantly. They drop because you are not addicted to pleasure any more. You have found something that makes you stop thinking in terms of comfort and start thinking in terms of freedom. Pleasure is addictive; pain is liberating and life is a perfect blend of the two.

The taste of wisdom contained by suffering is what frees us from the mundane flavors of this world. In one of our sacred books, it is written that wisdom is what an enlightened being eats and drinks. It is his staple food. We consume so much of the mundane because we have not yet developed a taste for the subtle delicacies of this existence. Things like compassion are for us like music is for the plants and animals; there is a spiritual gap that makes an interaction impossible. The compassionate ones find themselves dealing with a very helpless kind of predicament when their words fall upon deaf ears and their love bounces off the walls of ignorance. We need to evolve in order to perceive the true richness of the life we have been living all these incarnations.

When someone gets addicted to food, he loses interest in the blue sky and the sunset. When someone gets addicted to sex, he loses interest in food. When someone gets addicted to drugs, he loses interest in sex and when someone gets enlightened, he loses interest in drugs. Our consciousness gives up something only when it has got a better option. There is no other way to convince a consciousness and this is why many of the de-addiction programs fail to produce encouraging results. We ask the addicts to give up their greatest pleasure without offering them meditation and all the spiritual incentives that come with it. We are unable to cope with the emptiness which got a person addicted to something in the first place. The consciousness cannot be fooled. It follows a very simple and straight logic. It clings to the best it has tasted so far. Our consumptions clearly point towards our priority list in terms of pleasure.

A person addicted to heroin can give up his social status for it, his family for it, his profession for it, his health for it and even his morality for it. Why? Because the pleasure of being one with the cosmos can negate all our pains. But what an addict fails to see is that all his pains are waiting for him to come down from his "High" and with every passing day they are surmounting. He fails to see the limitation of psychedelics. We all fail to see the limitation of our pleasures and the handicaps of our body, mind and senses. What we need to know is that the body, mind and senses are merely tools to get in touch with Bliss; they are not bliss itself. Our pleasures are also merely a glimpse of the real thing; not the thing itself. The day we come to truly realize the potential of our consumptions, is the day we stop investing our being in them. Thereafter, we consume to live and not live to consume.

If you take a look at your daily routine you will find that you have subconsciously designed it with the pleasures in your life. Most of our office going fellow beings have got cups of tea or coffee scattered all over their routine to maintain their alertness and attitude. The ones with very challenging jobs have got an evening of hard drink to look forward to. We try to strike a balance between, that which we have to endure in order to survive and that which we have got, to keep our zest for life from falling below the lower threshold. This balancing can be very tricky if we don't know how to process our pain and suffering into wisdom. The facts of life, especially death and departure are too big to be handled by fleeting celebrations and intoxications. There has to be something spacious enough to accommodate all the paradoxes of life.

In spite of all our consumptions, we are never fulfilled because the stomach of our senses cannot be filled with vibrations of pleasure. The senses are always hungry. After they have had food, they want a desert. After they have had a desert, they want something else. We keep on feeding them and never take the time to ponder over the hopelessness of the situation we are trapped in. We live our incarnations chasing pleasures and die without having experienced real satisfaction. That which is beyond the recreations of our body, mind and senses remains unknown and un-experienced. We are unable to pull ourselves away from the noise of temptations and get acquainted with the silence of pure consciousness. We are unable to sacrifice our flavors for something that is absolutely tasteless in the beginning and hold on tenaciously to our various addictions. Our tiny pleasures, is all that we have got and renouncing them would be, for us, like renouncing life itself. To an ordinary man, renunciation sounds like pulling a baby away from its mother's breast. We suck our pleasures just the way a baby sucks milk. But we need to grow and expand.

Our aloneness often overpowers us and forces us to consume something or the other. We are not comfortable with being alone. It reminds us of our physical ailments, body aches, energy depletion, emotional battles and spiritual home-works. By giving our senses something to play with, we distract ourselves. All the pains are still there but we are able to temporarily forget them. It's like the pigeon closing its eyes when pounced upon by the cat. We don't dare to deal with our aloneness and just try to evade it for the time being. This is the basic difference between an ordinary man and an ascetic. The ascetic has decided to work on the core lack of his being and not play hide and seek with the major spiritual issues any more. Our aloneness is not something to run away from; it is the key with which to unlock the greatest secrets of this universe. Instead of consuming things, we should meditate and cultivate a healthy relationship with the silence of the cosmos.

The fragile thread that connects us with the silence we are surrounded by is snapped off every time we consume something. Whether it is the boosting of a self esteem and emotional energy by nicotine and caffeine or the altering of consciousness by drugs of all sorts, whether it is the experience of a sexual "High" or the pleasure of eating, the senses and the mind are always a noise of vibrations that shatters the silence of our communion with our source. The spiritual experiences induced by drugs are very violent for both the body and the mind. One quick look at the life of a heroin addict will tell you the price they pay for their ecstasies. There is a soft way to deepen and strengthen our bond with that which exists beyond the mind and which every soul craves to fall back into.

Meditation is, in a way, the cultivation of stillness through the consumption of silence. We become what we feed upon. So, when we feed upon the serenity of the universe, it becomes our experience. The silent wisdom which runs the cosmos starts seeping into our being. We become the recipients of a teaching that needs no words. The fabric of life unfolds before us in the form of intelligent and perfect disciplines that are beyond the grasp of an ordinary mind and a beauty that is invisible to the ordinary eye reveals itself. The world, as we know it, is a deafening noise of chases, hunts, conflicts and clashes. The power of silence and the power of the moment are unknown to the ordinary man. We are all living a horizontal life; the vertical dimension is missing. But the rare few, who eat and drink silence, are less likely to be found feeding their senses with the stuff of this world. What they seek is solitude; the canvas on which silence can be painted.

The drug addicts may have earned a bad name because of being totally unproductive for the rest of the society but the fact is that we are all addicted to something or the other. The chemistry of our brain is such that it gets hooked to anything that is consumed for a considerable period. Just as our body needs food, water and air to survive, the brain has its own foods, without which, it cannot function normally. Anyone who is addicted to caffeine knows that without its daily dose of the substance, the mind turns sluggish and disoriented. When you have had your morning cup of tea or coffee for decades, it has become a switch for the brain. Without it, the brain will behave like an electrical appliance without a supply of electricity. The secretions of hormones are linked to each other in such a way that if you disturb the chain at any point, the whole balance is disturbed. This is why it is very essential to befriend the body as well as the mind in order to win the battle of addiction. Instead of shocking our metabolism, we should assist it in getting back to normal without the support of a chemical from the outside. We have to help it produce everything from within.

It is only the consciousness that does not need to consume anything. The body needs foods and drinks, the mind needs chemicals and drugs, the senses need an expression or gratification. But the consciousness is self-sufficient; it needs nothing from the outside. It is for this reason that drugs which introduce us to pure consciousness and allow us to stay in that realm for some time are almost worshipped by those who have had enough of the nagging demands of the senses; the desires. Pure consciousness is revered and sought because an absence of hungers is one of its salient features. There are many who totally neglect all the other realities or even sacrifice them for it, such is the rejoicing of the soul having discovered it. There is an element of fatigue in serving the body, mind and senses which is exhausting the whole mankind and making many of us to look upon death as a relief. Pure consciousness provides us with a better option.

The nature of the mind is incessant thinking and the nature of senses is incessant hunger. When we are trapped inside these and identify with them, we are guaranteed to be tortured. No matter how many inventions are made and how many products are there in the market to be consumed by us, we cannot get fulfillment from serving our senses. Our eyes become tired of looking at temptations but our senses still want to see. Our stomach is full but our senses still want to eat. Our ears stop responding to the subtleties of frequency but our senses still want to listen. Our metabolism is tired of processing the various chemicals we are addicted to but our senses still keep on asking for more. Serving the senses is extremely tiring. But rarely someone wakes up to this truth. Most of us surrender to our habits instead of surrendering to God and spend our entire incarnation trying to make our nagging desires happy.

The life of common man is a spiritual dilemma; he wants to be happy but by consuming. It is as if you want to fly but without losing your contact with the ground. Used as a means to an end, our body, mind and senses are the greatest tools; in fact the only tools we have got to evolve to a higher level of being but used as an end in themselves they are frustratingly incapable of introducing us to the experience of ultimate freedom. This dilemma is the reason why we have intense consumptions like heroin on one hand and an immense misery on the other. Just as our body cannot lift the weight that an elephant can lift, we cannot force our brain chemistry into real enlightenment by consuming a psychedelic. After having our glimpses of heaven, we have to come back to the ordinary plane of reality and the contrast can be very painful for the soul. Dealing with this contrast is all that de-addiction is about.

The commercial world encourages the consumer in us by promising us happiness and we easily fall into the trap. According to a survey done recently, an average American citizen watches 34 hours of television per week and we all know that a great part of it is advertisements. If we could simply meditate for 34 hours in a week, instead of watching a television or sitting in front of a laptop and consuming unnecessary information, we could lay down the foundation of a new era. May be because it is so simple, it is difficult to understand. Unless and until man consciously steps out of all the traps he is born into, he cannot realize his true potential and without meditating, we cannot cultivate consciousness. Meditation is the only real cure for this ailing world. The consumer in us needs to be discouraged and the anchor of God in us needs to be known. Both these efforts have to be made simultaneously because they complement each other. Our belief in "Consuming for Happiness" has to be discarded but not through an artificial renunciation. It has to come out of an authentic wisdom like a leaf comes out of the branch of a tree.

The Challenge

The noise of all these meaningless thoughts has robbed me of my peace,
I seek the silence which is not disturbed by the trumpets of the mind.
The winds of change that blow everyday distract me from my purpose,
My wisdom gets carried away by the powerful pushes and pulls of the
  world.

I try to protect my reasoning from the violent invasions of ignorance,
But there are moments when it is blinded by the explosions of pent up rage.
My compassion is at the mercy of my own capacity to forgive,
I really don't know how much to bear and when to fight for my rights.

The paradoxes of life make me walk on a rope, balancing with the staff of
  truth,
Beyond the good, bad, right and wrong, the clarity of my vision waits for
  me.
I often lose my oneness in the tornadoes of duality,
These powerful forces provoke me into choosing "This" or "That."

At times it is so difficult to deal with the people in this world,
That silence seems to be the only way to create some space for sanity.
In the quietness of my solitude I look at all the dilemmas of my life,
And seek instruction from the parent truth, the truth that guides as all.

When the mud of my thoughts has settled down and my perception is clear
  and clean,
I know what is good for all of us and how we can help it bloom.

●●●●●●●●●●●●●●●●●●●●●●●●●●●●●●●

CHAPTER 2 - OUR INVISIBLE BEING

I have decided to use the words "Invisible Being" to share my inventions with all of you and I will be using the word "Soul" very sparingly so that my work does not suffer at the hands of terminology. When I use the word soul, it would mean the very root of life in us or in other words, the seat of our deepest connection with our source. In the Indian sacred texts, the soul is referred to as "Atman" and God is referred to as "Param Atman" or universal soul. A book on spirituality cannot be written, without a mention of this part of our being, quite a few times. Yet, the way it is used, does not give us an exact idea of what it is. In conversations, we use it even more vaguely and our best understanding of it is that it is that part of us which is invisible and which leaves our body at the time of death. But the spiritual phenomenon that I am trying to explain in this book demands a very deep understanding of all the participants that take part in the happening of it.

Since all which leaves the body at the time of death is our invisible being only, we can conclude that its four major components are mind, senses, Kleshas and awareness. At any particular moment our energy withdraws itself from one component and invests itself in the other. When we play chess, it is invested in the mind; when we are having a meal, it is invested in the senses; when we are distracted by one of the Kleshas, it is invested in that Klesha and when we meditate it is invested in awareness. To a large extent, this fluidity is provided to it by our breathing. If you hold the breath, the energy becomes immobile. If you stop breathing, the link between the body and the soul is snapped. If we take our body as hardware, then our invisible being is the software in it and breathing the electric supply. No two of them can operate without the third and they all go into the making of what we are.

The separation of the individual soul from the universal soul is the basis of Karma and reincarnation. Without this separation, our incarnation cannot have an individuality or debts to pay. We bind Karma because of this breakup of the substance into individual molecules or you can say the universal soul into individual souls. It is as if the existence throws us away from itself and then lays down before us a path to find our way back home. There is something very weird about the dance of life and all the paradoxes which make it possible. For example, imagine how many kilometers a seeker travels in search of a meaning and where he finally finds it. It is not surprising that the first thing many of those who got enlightened did was – to laugh at their own error of judgment regarding bliss.

Vibrations and frequencies is the form in which our invisible being manifests itself and interacts with the laws of the universe such as the law of attraction though this is a very over-simplified way of describing something that can change bodies and travel through all the realms of reality. For the existence, we are not these bodies and these names; we are packets of energy which vibrates. It responds to the truth of our vibrations. So, whether we are using our mind to think about something or absorbed in a sensuous experience or meditating to cultivate awareness, for the cosmos it all gets reduced to a cloud of vibrations. The infinite intelligence has its own way of simplifying all that appears to be highly complicated and mysterious. The characteristics of the elements that have been assembled together to make a human being are a way to knowing the mind of God. Our invisible being is characterized by the preservation of our immortality. Another characteristic of the invisible being is that it becomes the size of the body it is assigned. In an ant, it becomes the size of an ant; in an elephant, it becomes the size of an elephant. From head to toe and in every cell of the body, it is there. If the thumb of our feet is pricked with a needle, the mind, the senses and the awareness, all become occupied with the experience of pain and the need to do something about it. Because, for our invisible being, every pain is a call for help and an urgency to be dealt with. Our whole body is soaked in it like a sponge soaked in water. The mind and the senses are very strongly linked together and work in unison. If we are watching a programme on the television and our mind is thinking about something else, minutes of it can totally go unnoticed and we are unable to recall what we missed. So, that means the eyes are not enough to see; the mind also has to be there. Similarly, those who don't eat mindfully are unable to enjoy their meal. Now the element that jells together, the mind, senses and Kleshas is - awareness. If we take it away, they all fall apart. It is this ability of awareness or consciousness to distance itself from the other three components, which makes it possible for us to free ourselves of the clutches of the Kleshas, mind and senses and to be able to use them for our purpose instead of being used by them. When you step away from them and entrench yourself in consciousness, they are like your hands and feet; connected to you, part of you but at a manageable distance.

It is because of the amalgamation of mind and Kleshas that every time the Kleshas ask for something, the mind tries to rationalize their demand. Without an awareness to watch over them, the situation could be very tricky. For example, when anyone who is addicted to caffeine, feels like having a cup of tea or coffee, the mind immediately says, "Yes why not? It has got a lot of antioxidants and is the perfect drink for creativity to pour out of us." The mind rationalizes the urge. But awareness says, "Now wait a minute; too much of caffeine is acidic for our digestion and irritates the lining of the stomach as well as the intestines." The mind and the Kleshas are like two naughty kids; the consciousness is like a wise and compassionate parent. At times, it becomes the third kid and starts playing with them; at times, it pulls itself away from them and refuses to participate in the game. Without consciousness, they cannot go on. Hence all the politics we play with our own self; trying to seduce the consciousness into agreeing with the desires of the Kleshas and the rationalizations of the mind.

Now let us look at sleep from the perspective of these four basic components. The occurrence of a nocturnal discharge as a result of dreams in which we are involved in sexual activity proves that our Kleshas and the subconscious mind are awake or active. But since we often do things in a dream that we would not do when we are awake, there is certainly not enough awareness to check the Kleshas, also called Vikaars, Doshas, Agnis or Panch Chors. So the conscious mind and most of the consciousness itself are both sleeping. There is something in a dream which appears to be awareness but it is actually our sense of identity, our ego. It is the one which tries to keep the things as they are during the day or during our waking hours and makes us behave in a way which synchronizes with our image; our virtual self. The consciousness or awareness is in such a restful state that if a candled is brought close to one of our body parts, our senses and the subconscious mind will create a dream in which that body part encounters a fire or something hot. This certifies the depth of our rest and also the components which are active during sleep.

The Kleshas, though powerful enough to have written the history of mankind, cannot do anything unless they win over, first the mind and then the consciousness or awareness. With every success, they gain power and momentum and become capable of carrying out an act. Because we are oblivious to the whole process, we are unable to see the buildup of things. Most of the time we become aware of something after it has already happened. But whatever it is, the mind does not exhibit any preference for either the Kleshas or the awareness - the mind always takes a neutral stance. If you identify with your awareness, it serves the awareness; if you identify with your Kleshas, it serves the Kleshas.

The five senses of sight, sound, smell, taste and touch are the doors through which information regarding the existence around us steps into our being. They are the input channels. If we compare our mind to an ocean of information, then our five senses can be compared to the rivers that fall into it and contribute their waters.

For every object known to us, there is information in our mind about it and it comes from all the experiences we have had of that object. A single look at an image of the object or the object itself opens up a closet in our mind and corresponding thoughts start pouring out of the closet. If one of our Kleshas can associate itself with these thoughts, a pattern is formed. Once formed, a pattern has the tendency to maintain itself by feeding on thoughts of the same kind.

Now, the closets in our mind can be opened by imagination also. If you think about someone of the opposite sex with your eyes closed, the thoughts can create a virtual image in the mind and this virtual image can open the corresponding closet. The thoughts which pour out of the closet trigger the Klesha of lust and thus, a pattern is formed. Once formed, it will try to maintain itself by feeding on thoughts of the same kind. Similarly, the presence of someone we don't like or even the imagination of that person, opens a closet by that name in our mind and the thoughts that pour out of it trigger our ego, anger and jealousy. Without an awareness of these patterns, an intervention is not possible. But the one who can see this chain can break it at any point and then replace it with something better.

The more we cling to the past, the more closets we have in our mind and the more crowded it gets. In the language of the computers, we can say that clinging to the past is like clinging to folders and files containing nothing more than a data. The part of our mind other than the senses is very much like a computer. Just as a computer slows down if too much space in its memory is taken and unnecessary files are not deleted, our mind also cannot function properly if we hold on to too many of unnecessary memories, views, habits of thinking, fears and phobias. A freshness of the mind plays a very significant role in cultivating awareness. If the mind is too heavy, it becomes a load for the consciousness. Any one component of the soul can easily affect the rest of them. The ideal way to evolve is to cultivate awareness, keep the mind fresh, use senses only for healthy inputs and purify the Kleshas with self - control and wisdom.

Since the senses are there in every cell of our body, in some form or the other, and are an extension of the mind only, we come to the conclusion that there is mind in every cell of our body. A very simple way of verifying this is that if you are involved in some kind of mental labor, your feet also experience the fatigue and if the feet are massaged, the head is relaxed. The head no doubt is the central location or the head quarters of the mind due to the brain being there, but the mind is actually much more than all that can be measured detected and photographed by the scientific instruments. The secretions in the brain, the allocation of its different parts to specific functions, the nature of brain waves and its response to different stimuli provided through the senses can be studied in a scientific laboratory but there is one element which goes totally unnoticed - the consciousness. It is the element which makes all the difference between the mind of an ordinary man and the mind of a Buddha. If we study the brain of a Buddha in a scientific environment, we cannot detect, measure or photograph his enlightenment. In the simplest words, mind is brain plus the miraculous senses and the living consciousness.

Consciousness or awareness is for the senses, Kleshas and mind, what breath is for the blood that flows in our veins. You take it away and everything collapses like a house of cards. Without consciousness, the ear cannot hear, the eyes cannot see, the nostrils cannot smell, the tongue cannot taste and the skin cannot feel a touch. An easy way of knowing this is by eating something while listening to a great piece of music through the headphones. You will find that because of the awareness being pulled in two different directions, the experience of both the food and the music gets diluted. Similarly, whenever you experience lust at the sight of a tempting picture of the opposite sex, pull your awareness away from the trio of eyes, mind and the Klesha of "Kaam", and watch how all the three of them go back to where they belong. They cannot conspire without it. Without awareness, the eyes will be reduced to a lens and a retina, the lust will be dispersed into the vastness of consciousness and the mind will be unable to hold on to thoughts or thought patterns.

We all have an awareness. But it is not established in itself. It is not available to itself. It is like someone who is so busy helping and serving others that he has no time left for himself. We identify so intensely with our mind and Kleshas that our awareness gets reduced to something that has been conquered and enslaved and has got no voice of its own. Our Kleshas dictate our being and dominate both the mind and the consciousness. They can easily get the mind and consciousness into agreement over their gratification. Within seconds, all the rest of our soul is completely in harmony with any of our Klesha that has got triggered by a situation or stimulus and we are like an arrow pulled back to the maximum; ready to be shot. Most of our actions pour out of a state of unconsciousness.

Now, I have been frequently referring to the term "Klesha" while trying to explain the way different components of our invisible being interact with each other and I feel the need to elaborate on that. The literal meaning of the word Klesha is - "Lack of harmony". The ancient sages discovered through meditation, forms of energy which threw them out of their space of consciousness and disturbed their peace. The number of these invisible forces varies from text to text but they all agree on the five major ones - Kaam (Lust), Krodh (Anger), Lobh (Greed), Moh (Attachment) and Ahankar (Ego). If we include the minor ones, the count can go up to 30. But for all practical purposes, five are enough. Almost every sacred text calls these energies by a different name, depending upon the language of the source of its wisdom. The Upanishads speak of five fires (Panch Agni), the Pali texts call them "Nivaranas" (Hindrances), the Yoga sutra refers to them as Panch Kleshas (Defilements) and the holy book of Sikhs mentions them as Panch Chor (Five Thieves), Panch Dokh (Five Ailments), Kilbikh (impurities) or Panj Vikars (Five Weaknesses). The purpose of the name we chose is to make it easy for us to recognize these miraculous creations and then share our insights with others. It has absolutely nothing to do with what they are. I have chosen the word "Klesha" simply because it best describes my own experience of these powerful enemies of spiritual harmony.

If we were to describe the nature of energy that the chief components of our invisible being are, Kleshas are an energy that has got great conquering power, mind is the one that can process information and consciousness is an energy that is aware of itself. The distinction between these elements of our being is the secret of the dance we dance and the songs we sing. Those who reside in the Kleshas, live a life of violent gratifications. Those who reside in the mind, are always busy processing information and those who reside in awareness, live a conscious life. The Kleshas cannot think, the mind cannot conquer; hence the internal mutiny. It is only consciousness that has got the ability to govern the rest of our being in a graceful manner. As energy, it is more mature than the hungers of the Kleshas and the thoughts of the mind and can therefore see through their tricks, games and traps. For the mind, there is a lot that is opaque but for the consciousness, everything is transparent. Consciousness can be called the crown of our being. It can create order out of chaos by placing things where they belong. The mind cannot do that when it comes to the distractions within. It can be easily overpowered by them. But awareness, when fully cultivated, can declare itself as the master of the senses, mind and Kleshas.

Now the term used to describe the five organs of perception viz. eyes, ears, nose, tongue and skin, in spiritual texts, is "Gyan Indriyas". Indriya is a Sanskrit term and denotes tentacles extended by the mind and consciousness to interact with the universe. It is through the Indriyas that the universe impresses itself upon the mind and it is through them that the mind expresses itself. The total number of Indriyas is ten. We have five Gyan Indriyas and five Karm Indriyas. Gyan Indriyas are the organs of perception and Karm Indriyas are the organs of action. The five Karm Indriyas are mouth, hands, legs, anus and genitals. Put simply, the Gyan Indriyas are entrance gates for perception while Karm Indriyas are the exit gates for action or expression. An understanding of the Indriyas and control over them plays a very significant role in expanding the gap between the external stimuli and our response to them. Understanding and awareness convert a tennis ball into a football. We are able to see more clearly and can handle the invisibles more efficiently.

Through the organs of perception, an external stimulus is transported by the senses to the mind and then very frequently, by thoughts to one of the Kleshas. If we are conscious enough, we can stop it right there and kill the monster while it's small because once triggered, a Klesha has its own momentum which is often quite tough to handle. Its' energy has a numbing effect on our alertness and can be very overwhelming to tackle. In the Bhagwad Geeta, it is mentioned that if the senses are very sharp and acute, they carry away the minds of even good "Sadhaks" i.e. practitioners impetuously, just as the gale carries away the ship in stormy weather. The energy of a Klesha is like an emotional storm; it can easily sweep of its feet, a soul that is not firmly rooted in awareness. When we identify with the mind or the Kleshas, we cannot be firmly rooted. Hence our spiritual vulnerability and the dominance of Kleshas in the world we live in.

The mind and the senses are fatigued by the bombardment that comes from the stimuli of the world but the Kleshas never tire. They are either dormant or hungry or satisfied but never tired. This makes them all the more powerful. If you have two people wrestling with each other and the stamina of one of them is infinite, you can be sure of who is going to win the bout. When we haven't cultivated an awareness yet and try to take down a Klesha with just the mind, we are destined to lose. As soon as the mind is exhausted, the Klesha is going to overpower. To win the battle against Kleshas, you have to entrench yourself in awareness. There is no need to fight; just watching the enemy and understanding its mannerism is enough. The kleshas are like darkness and awareness is like a torch; simply moving it across the components of our being is enough.

Then why is self - mastery so difficult? It's so because awareness becomes a torch of illumination only when it has been cultivated enough. The utility of wheat cannot be expected from wheatgrass. When it is not developed enough, it is merely something that blends together the senses, the mind and the Kleshas. Just as a child can be manipulated by an adult, the awareness of an ordinary man can be manipulated by the trio of senses, mind and Kleshas. Our education systems are totally based upon the cultivation of mind and earning a living; there is hardly anything for the development of consciousness and the divine purpose of our incarnation. The word meditation is not heard in either the schools or the colleges and universities. This is the fundamental cause of mass unconsciousness. Where do you think is the awareness of a common man? Why is his behavior so lacking in it?

The awareness of a common man is like a small child living with three adults. It is completely undeveloped and a toy for them to play with. Through their extensive use, the senses, mind and Kleshas are developed much more in comparison to the consciousness. It can therefore be easily maneuvered. This fourth component of our invisible being becomes known to us as a separate entity only when we extricate it from the other three and define it for ourselves with spiritual practices. To the world that we live in, it is something like "The Missing element". A minimum amount of consciousness is no doubt necessary, without which an ordinary person can't even drive a car on a highway but most of us never take it beyond that bare minimum. We stop at that which is enough for us to operate in this world; the functional alertness. To declare its mastery over the agility of the senses, the brilliance of the mind and the power of the Kleshas, our alertness needs to be developed into a super - consciousness. Nothing less than that would be of much spiritual significance and nothing less than that would be able to liberate us.

The quality of consciousness we have, decides the quality of being we are. The difference between an ordinary fraud and a man of compassion is that of consciousness. Senses, mind and Kleshas are simply instruments which our being uses to express itself. Even a thief has got enough awareness to go on with his theft without being caught, but he is not aware of what he is doing as a human being to another human being. Corruption, at its very core, is not a social, economic or political problem; it is a spiritual problem. If we are not conscious enough, we are bound to be corrupt in one way or the other. Our perception of reality depends upon the quality of our consciousness and when it has not been evolved all that we perceive is duality, lack and the fear of death. In other words, we are what we are because of what we are unable to perceive. Our consciousness is, in a way a signature of our understanding of the cosmos.

The door to higher wisdom opens only when consciousness is withdrawn from the other three components of our invisible being, established in itself and allowed to feed on the cosmic energy. This is what meditation is all about and our identification with the senses, mind or Kleshas is the greatest hindrance to the objective of meditation. Without extricating the awareness which is invested in these three, we cannot create for ourselves, a platform from where we can observe the rest of our self and without an observation point we cannot take a leap into the less known dimensions of reality. The mass unconsciousness of the world we live in is basically due to the investment of the consciousness of individuals in their Kleshas, senses and mind. We have got a lot of intelligence and sensuality on our planet, but very little consciousness. The minds are highly developed, the senses are highly sharpened and the Kleshas are like hungry ghosts but the consciousness appears to have become extinct like the dinosaurs. Awareness would never have created a world that is almost destined to self destruct.

Now, the four components of our invisible being are like its limbs; its hands and feet. The one we use develops; the one we don't remains undeveloped. The mind of an illiterate farmer is not as developed as that of a scientist. The sense of hearing of an ordinary man is not as developed as that of a sound engineer or someone who mixes and masters music tracks. Of our Kleshas, the one we feed the most, encourage the most and express the most, becomes the signature of our being and our energy is inclined to flow towards its gratification very frequently. So, unless we use our awareness in our daily routine, it is not going to develop. Unless we design our day in such a way that a few hours are dedicated to the cultivation of consciousness, it will remain a fog of mystery for us and never take the shape of an element with definite characteristics.

The being of an ordinary man is like a fog of confusion; the being of a Yogi has well formed and well defined components. The science of spirituality is in fact, the science of internal organizing through understanding, detachment and the realization of our false identifications. The Yogi knows exactly what he is and what he is not; the common man doesn't. If you spend some time figuring out the cause of chaos in our world, you will be surprised to find that it is the chaos inside our individuals. The world we live in is exactly a projection of the minds we are surrounded by. If it is ugly, the minds that have made it cannot be beautiful and the mind can never be beautiful without its liberation from the Kleshas. In the absence of a cultivated consciousness, the Kleshas are an affliction for the mind. Hungry desires torture the mind by pulling it in directions that lead us away from the source of our being. The soul longs for its source and the way back home is consciousness; it is not the mind and senses; it is not the Kleshas.

Another way of looking at our invisible being is looking at it through the eyes of a quantum physician and when we do so, it is nothing but energy. When the consciousness invested in the senses, mind and Kleshas is extricated, this energy becomes available to us and it lays down the foundation for self healing and self realization. If this energy is offered to the mind, it will convert it into thoughts, most of which will be useless and disempowering. If it is offered to the Kleshas, they will use it as a food for their gratification. But when this energy is offered to awareness, it is utilized for recuperation, regeneration, evolution and expansion.

When we feel depleted of energy, it is so because we have been continuously spending it on either thoughts and emotions or the feeding of the senses. All methods and techniques of relaxing are, basically, learning how to move away from the mind, senses and Kleshas. When you separate yourself from the body, mind and breath and establish yourself as the witness, you are actually moving towards pure consciousness; the "No-Mind" dimension of our being. It's the dimension most in tune with the cosmic energy and therefore the secret to all kinds of healing. But to reap its benefits, we have to develop it to the level where it becomes our new identity. We have to stop identifying ourselves with our body, mind, senses and Kleshas and start knowing ourselves as just a consciousness.

We can use the consciousness as a participant in our karmic action, we can use it as a torch of illumination or we can also use it as an energy aware of itself. When we are just drifting through our daily routine, our consciousness is merely a participant in our actions. When we concentrate and focus on something in particular, inside us or outside, it becomes a beam of awareness. When we extricate it from the body, mind, senses and Kleshas and establish it in itself, it matures into an energy that is aware of everything in general but not something in particular. From here, it can take a leap into higher dimensions of reality, provided we can keep it there for long enough and not let it step down into the thickness of our incarnation.

Just as the object in focus of a torch is surrounded by darkness, focused consciousness is surrounded by a lot of unconsciousness. When we concentrate our attention on something, there is a lot that we have to become oblivious to. The focusing of consciousness is termed as "Ekagrata" in the Indian texts. It is essential for getting us introduced to the nature of mind and the distractions within because only when you try to concentrate, you become aware of how hard it is to hold on to one pattern of thinking. Focusing makes your mind more powerful and capable of deep diving into the mysteries of the cosmos. All great scientists made their achievements through the practice of this technique. But it is not the same thing as pure consciousness which is called "Chaitanya" in the spiritual texts. "Ekagrata" is - awareness of something while "Chaitanya" is - just awareness. When you are focusing your attention, you are still in the mind only but when you are "Just Aware" you have stepped out of the mind.

An absence of thought is the simplest way to describe the nature of pure consciousness though this definition is negative in the use of words. And when there are no thought patterns, the illumination of the awareness is like the light of a lamp or the sky at dusk and dawn. There is no focused beam; just a uniform field of energy that knows. For a consciousness fully established in itself, the mind, senses and Kleshas are simply instruments with which it can create its unique symphonies. When you have no control over them, the elements of your being are like musical instruments that are out of tune. No music can be created out of them. But when you establish yourself in pure consciousness, everything has a role to play in the song of your soul. The one who resides in absolute consciousness does not see the body, mind, senses and Kleshas as distractions; he sees them as beautiful tools to assist him in dancing the dance of life. The existence reaches out to you through them and you reach out to the existence through them. They are like an embrace between you and the cosmos.

Establishing your consciousness in itself is like landing on moon; the gravitational pull of the world on you is reduced to one sixth. You don't get sucked in by all the "Irresistible Temptations" around you and you can look at the lawful unfolding of everything in your life without personalizing it. From here, when you witness the mind, senses and Kleshas you find that they are exactly what they are supposed to be and they could not have been better. You realize that the problem was not them being what they are; the problem was, you identifying yourself with them and then assuming that they are you and you are them.

••••••••••••••••••••••••••••••••••••••

CHAPTER 3 - BEYOND THE COMPLEXITY OF RELATIONSHIPS

Relating

The love I receive nourishes my soul,
The hatred teaches me to tolerate and forgive;
The strange paradoxes of the life I contain,
Force me into an expansion I need.

The ones who love me make me bloom,
The ones who do not make me wise;
The ways of God are beyond my grasp,
There is always something that I don't yet know.

My heart is the centre of my own universe,
And my feelings are the strings that hold it together;
I know that without compassion around it,
Wisdom can be very cold and insensitive.

The souls that provide me with a reason to live,
Are the ones who can understand the language of love;
Together we share this secret of God,
This jewel in the crown of the life we have got.

The freeing of a soul from the lower elements,
Gives me a joy I can't explain;
I love to see the blooming of a heart,
And all that I say being understood by someone.

The pearl of compassion becomes all the more valuable,
When it finds its place in the ornaments of brotherhood;
The darkness of the world when cured by light,

Lays down the foundation for a way to be together.

Man does not tire because of the work he has to do to feed himself and his family; he tires because of the effort he has to make to keep the different relationships in his life going. Dealing with the subtleties of relating with another human being can prove to be the toughest part of an incarnation. The ones that are harmonious can provide our life with the greatest purpose, drive and ambition while the ones that lack harmony can take all the meaning out of it. We are all in fact a product of the relationships in our life – both positive and negative and our priorities are decided by the way we balance this scale.

We have physical needs, emotional needs and spiritual needs. The one whose physical needs are not fulfilled has little regard for emotion and spirituality. The poor man who does not even have sufficient food, clothing and shelter has no place in his heart for relationships and God. To give and receive love and to relate with others of our kind, we have to have our most fundamental needs fulfilled. When we have got enough to eat, an adequate house to live in and an income to take care of our basic expenditures, our emotional and spiritual cravings start dominating our mind by seeking a gratification. Relating with other human beings and relating with our source is an intrinsic part of our very biological makeup. It is not just something that we learn from the society or our parents and relatives.

We love relationships because they make us feel alive. When one consciousness interacts with another, they both include each other and expand. This expansion makes us feel alive. In aloneness, we contract. In aloneness, we shrink and hibernate. Aloneness is like a safe cave that protects us from emotional burnouts but if you spend all the time with yourself, your personality becomes stagnant and your views become rigid. We need to interact with others to keep the life force in us flowing and to maintain our flexibility since flow and flexibility represent life. Even enlightened beings do not spend all the time alone though their relationship with themselves is their most valued possession. They love being with others because it is in this get-together that their wisdom and insights find an optimum utilization. Just as a delicious dish is of any value only if there is someone to eat, wisdom is also of any value to the mankind only if it brings hope and light to those of us who are struggling with despair and darkness.

The dance of life derives its momentum from "One" showing up as "many", interacting with each other and falling back into "One". The ones we love pull us out of our separation and duality. We embrace discomfort and sacrifice with a smile for those that are precious to us. Our relationships are the primary factor that designs the fundamental fabric of our incarnation. Whatever we are, we are, because of the souls we have adored and cherished and the souls we have suffered from. Each and every one of us is being sculptured on a daily basis by the chisels of love and hatred. The course of our incarnation is decided by people who love and support us and people who hate and oppose us. The harmony and the disharmony in our life, blend together in a very mysterious way, to assist our consciousness in rising above all the paradoxes.

If you take a quick look at your own spiritual evolution, you will be really surprised to find that you grew the most while trying to accommodate in your consciousness the ones who made you suffer the most. That is, in fact, the major portion of the secret called "Suffering Is Grace". God comes to us in the form of the good to make us happy; he comes to us in the form of the "Bad" and the "Ugly" to make us grow. Our spiritual muscles cannot grow from the lifting of weights that they have gotten used to. Our strength comes from overcoming the obstacles we face while living according to our core values. Characters like Guru Gobind Singh Ji, Prithvi Raj Chauhan, Maharana Pratap and Chhatrapati Shivaji were all born out of the company of innocent and child like souls. It was in protecting their principles and honor from oppression and cruelty that their inner strength surfaced and became a standard for the whole mankind to look up to.

Our incarnation expresses itself through our interactions with those that we care for and the ones we have to protect them from. It is in these interactions that our ideals can be found and it is through these interactions that our ideals get defined. Just as the shape of a rock is formed by the winds which blow against it, the character of a man is formed by those who try to make him offer his values in the service of their selfish interests. One of the deepest insights regarding relationships is that we depend upon our friends for the blooming of our compassion and we depend on our enemies for the defining of our character as well as the building up of our strength. The polarities of this existence including human incarnation appear to be negating each other, but in truth, they feed upon each other.

One of the most amazing aspects of relating with another human being, which I have discovered from my own personal experience, is that the fundamental chemistry of our relationship with another person can be found out within a few minutes of an interaction. This basic chemistry never changes. You can call it astrological, you can call it Karmic but the fact is that it is sponsored by God. I have tried to improve upon my relationship, with those that I don't get along with well, and after decades of wasted effort, I have finally come to the conclusion that it is not within my power to do so. If someone likes me, he or she likes me; if someone dislikes me, he or she dislikes me. If I like someone, I like him or her; if I dislike someone, I dislike him or her. An old prophet used to say, "If I can love you; Great! If you can love me; Great! If I cannot love you; I am helpless. If you cannot love me; you are helpless". I have finally realized that my job is not to improve upon relationships; my job is to find the ones that are harmonious and allow the ones that are not.

I have tried to probe into what it is that makes me compatible with some and incompatible with others so that I could at least explain it to myself, and I did find some rational explanations. But there is something quite irrational that lies beyond the capacity of my intellect and which never gets explained. We call it intuition and when it is really developed, your trust in it is so strong that weird behavior becomes routine for you and you don't even feel the need to explain your conclusions and decisions to the world. I like people who are loyal, honest, transparent and not selfish, but there is something in the ones who don't have to knock on the door of my spiritual heart, which cannot be put into words. It can only be felt and experienced. There is an element in my being which can sense it as acutely as the fragrance of a rose and through the years, I have come to trust its authenticity.

I have had relationships that lasted only for a few months and then faded out, I have had those that went fine for years and then reached a point where I could not afford to entertain them anymore, I have got relationships that run all the way through my childhood, adolescence and adulthood and have passed the test of time and I also have those that are so vast and powerful that I don't have to worry at all about spoiling them or causing them an irreparable damage. Relationships have, in fact, been my most potent vehicle for the inner transformation and also the point of contact between my soul and the rest of the existence. It was through them that I realized my spiritual poverty and it was through them that I experienced the heart of this cosmos i.e. compassion. It was through them that I suffered the pangs of duality and it was through them that I had the taste of oneness. They were the primary consideration behind all my major decisions in life and the most powerful force behind every course of action.

I have felt this existence just as much as I have thought about it and my life has been a strange blend of emotionality and intellect or you could say the intuitive heart and the rational mind. The character of people I come in contact with, whether on a daily basis, or once in a while, is the basic chisel that is sculpturing my being. Every interaction with someone forces me to look at myself from a different angle and makes me aware of the expectations that a particular role model has from me. Every time I brush against another consciousness, it wakes me up in one way or the other and pulls me out of spiritual laziness. I become conscious of my responsibilities and also those areas of my life which require my immediate attention. Because no matter where we start our conversations from, at some point during the table tennis of views, our primary concerns are almost guaranteed to surface. Conversations between souls are just like music; if the participants are in tune, they create a beautiful symphony and if they are out of tune all that you get is an emotional noise. If I had not tasted this harmony, I would have never known what it is but fortunately I have. And I have also experienced friction of the highest order. The contrast is what keeps me looking for, people I can be with, without having to protect my heart from an exploitation or invasion. I wish to live with a heart that is not afraid of the variations in human character and which does not lose its touch with compassion in spite of all the violence that is there in the world. My intuition tells me that a few beautiful souls can assist me in realizing this possibility.

When we talk about relationships I am reminded of the one who has done the greatest research on the fundamental chemistry of the twelve zodiacs – Astrologer Linda Goodman. If I had not read her work, I would never have been able to explain the attractions and repulsions I experienced while dealing with fellow beings. Having read "Star Signs" and "Love Signs" 20 years ago and then experiencing the truth of it in real life, I am convinced that just as the bringing together of Hydrogen and Oxygen under certain conditions results in the product called water, when we bring together people, they react with each other according to the principles of astrology. Though the spiritual evolution of an individual makes him more capable of accommodating differences and clashes and creates in him a space from where he can deal more effectively with attractions and aversions, the laws of astrology still apply on him like any other law. It is still something to be lived with. All that we can do is respect the law, understand it and use it to our advantage.

When you apply the wisdom of this realized woman, Linda Goodman, to the fabric of your own personal world, you can clearly see that the friction in our relationships is not something to be wrestled with; it is something to be allowed as divine will. Many of us waste a major portion of our incarnation fighting astrological chemistry. With the assumption that we can improve upon our relationships, by working on them rather than working on ourselves, we keep on trying to gain control over our helplessness. But at some point in our incarnation, we surrender to everything in our life which is not according to our taste and realize the true potency of the words, "Not my will but thy will be done". The density and complexity of emotional turmoil, in relationships which are not in harmony with our basic nature, is the thing that forces us to step out of our ego and start living from a space that makes it possible for us to see the lawful unfolding of life inside and outside us.

On the other hand, the experience of resonance in a relationship can be the most blissful experience of life. When two souls are in tune with each other, love can be expressed in its most beautiful forms. When we are compatible with someone, the togetherness is not a mathematical addition of two individualities; it is a mysterious multiplication of compassion. The environment of spiritual harmony can make it possible for us to expand beyond imagination and become one with the whole of cosmos. When we drop our defenses, embrace our vulnerability and open the doors of our heart, the whole existence could move into it. Certain conditions are necessary, for the spiritual explosion of compassion to occur in our being and a relationship of resonance happens to be, an ideal situation to start from. Not only does it give us a taste of the most precious thing that exists in this cosmos, it also provides us with the wisdom of a contrast which is essential for designing our incarnation.

Just as a plant starts losing the life in it if it doesn't get enough of water, air and sunlight, the compassion in us starts dying if we are deprived of the company of friendly souls. If you are surrounded by people who know nothing other than exploiting and manipulating, your emotional world is bound to become hard and dry. Love is the food that our soul needs to stay healthy and loyal companionship is the second major source of it, the first being our relationship with God. When two souls are in synchronization with each other, the resultant mastermind and the shared awareness acquire the status of a force which can move mountains. The difficult becomes easy, the impossible becomes possible and the incurable becomes curable. The energy that creates worlds, though in each and every one of us becomes most evident in an environment of emotional harmony and spiritual synchronization. Miracles are simply the music which comes from souls in tune with each other or in tune with the universal soul and where love is expressed and received without any reservation, everything gets healed.

When there's resonance between souls, the happiness of one becomes the smile of the other and the suffering of one becomes the desperation of the other. The personality becomes fluid and flexible; the identity loses its hard lines of definition. Then one serves the other not because of some social, spiritual or moral obligation but because that is the only thing which makes sense. There is no master and servant or the helper and helped; there is just a situation to be handled, a life to be lived, a moment to be shared or an experience to be had. When there is transparency in two pairs of eyes and the souls behind those eyes are committed to each other, life can express itself through dimensions unknown to those imprisoned in their cages of selfishness. The language of love can be spoken and heard by only those who have stepped out of their individuality and become available to the compassion which holds us all together.

The most prominent difference between friction in relationships and resonance in relationships is that in case of friction, we exclude and contract whereas in resonance we include and expand. We exclude by closing our spiritual heart; we include by opening it. In the company of those we love, there is nothing to defend and protect; there is nothing to keep us on guard. We can afford to allow them into our being just the way we allow a beautiful good mannered kid into our house. There is no fear of something getting stolen or something getting broken. An environment of trust and faith is there and it feels more comfortable than the greatest of worldly luxuries. From here, you can handle all the challenges of life without a frown and assist the whole world in moving towards peace, harmony, tolerance and compassion. The potential of love can neither be measured nor estimated. At the nucleus of the greatest of revolutions in history, you will always find a few childlike souls having fallen in love with each other.

Now, the pain of relationships that lack harmony is the intellectual and spiritual gap which cannot be bridged while the pain of those that are harmonious, is the impermanence which is a characteristic of life itself. It is this pain that compels the one who is living consciously, to seek refuge in the dimension of "Bairag". It's the space created in your being from the inclusion of worldly ignorance and impermanence in your consciousness. From here, when you relate with another soul, you are fully aware of the limitations of a human incarnation and the intricacies of the process of spiritual evolution. From here, you can handle individual differences, generation gaps, variations in human character, karmic complications and contradictions in belief systems, in a manner which protects your incarnation from the influence of life forces in their various forms.

Bairag

After being born to a family of peasants,
My contact with life was the people around me;
It was through them that I received my share,
Of the various emotions we can feel and express.

A lot of these souls were brave and honest,
So truth was there for me to feed upon;
 My father's father was a hardcore ascetic,
Who woke up at 1 every morning for his practice.

Time went by and some faces disappeared,
But soon I would be introduced to more of them;
I was too powerless to question anything,
All I could do was receive my share.

My bonds became stronger as I grew through the years,
The power of emotions dominated my being;
I felt more acutely the departures and arrivals,
And I could feel the sinking and blooming of my heart.

I felt this world more than I thought about it,
My heart had become the centre of my learning;
The purpose of my life was not known to me yet,
The wisdom of the sages had not yet dawned upon me.

But by the end of my fourth decade,
I could see the patterns of change everywhere;
The autumns were too strong for one heart to take,
And I had to find a new place to live in.

A place from where I could endure all the pain,
That comes with being human and dealing with dilemmas;
A place where I could hide from the insanity of the world,
In order to keep myself normal and sane.

A place which could not be invaded by desires,
Or the noise of the crowd or the tides of emotions;
A place which could not be pulled down or dragged,
Into the meaningless issues of ignorance.

A place that could stay as it is through the change,
And not be affected by the ups and downs;
From where I could see them all as one,
The pleasure and the pain, the loss and the gain.

A place where I could rest when I was shattered and tired,
When nothing in my life seemed to care for what I required;
When everyone around me seemed unfriendly and distant,
And the forces too hostile for one poor soul to endure.

The stubborn refusal of the less conscious, to listen to what you have to say, can easily freeze your compassion to death if you don't protect it with patience, calm and forgiveness. In one of the religious texts, forgiveness has been described as the house in which religion lives and anger the energy which can pollute it in a moment. Now, without having established yourself in the dimension of Bairag, it is not possible for you to either be patient or to forgive. If we are standing on one leg, we can easily be thrown out of balance. Discovering this space or touching this space is not enough for a spiritual stability; you have to be able to rest in it and then deal with the patterns of the world in an efficient way. It is easy to be calm and stable in aloneness but it is tough to maintain this perspective while interacting with others, especially the ones who have a very different view about how things are i.e. the reality.

There are people whom you have to keep at a safe distance for the good of your cause because if you don't, they are inclined to invade your space, interfere with your life in every possible way and injure your compassion. Now, the problem is that this contraction of your being could prove to be an ailment for the heart that is required for love to manifest. Your defenses against invasions could become so strong that even the well meaning find it hard to step into your emotional privacy. You could become so accustomed to your cave of introversion that the environment which liberates and awakens gets afflicted with fear and doubt. The solution to this problem can be found in accepting your vulnerability while living in faith. It is possible to maintain your distance, from ignorance too thick to seep into, and at the same time, keep your heart open for those who have not invested heavily in their ego and are good at perceiving the subtleties of emotions.

When you will look at relationships from the space I am referring to, you will see each and every soul choosing its own path and picking up its own tools to sculpture itself. The paths and tools in themselves can be so contradictory that they leave you with a very few people who share your vision or who you could hang out with on a regular basis. The directions in which your friends, relatives and acquaintances are moving can be so unique that there is hardly anything on the surface that seems common or that can be used as a point of intersection. When you add the peculiarity of individual karmic predicaments to that, it can amount to a great helplessness which forms the basis of your spiritual seclusion. The silence of "One" seems to be getting lost in the noise of the "Many" and you find yourself being thrown back into your own centre for guidance regarding the steering of your incarnation.

The conviction of a soul in the path it has chosen and the tools it has picked up for the designing of its universe, is so strong, that you see great compassion in not interfering with the plans and projects of others. In spite of all the good intentions for the ones you care for, you can feel a subtle violence in imposing your ideas and your vision on their perception of reality. You can see that they don't feel guided by your wisdom; they feel dictated instead. They feel robbed of the freedom to look at the world through their eyes, think about it with their mind and feel it with their senses. By the end of all this spiritual chess, you simply wish to live and let live. You just want to set everyone free and take your share of freedom by refusing to sign up as their caretaker. A lot of the warmth in your heart is replaced by a cold witnessing of the indifference demonstrated by the ignorant and the arrogant. But a cold and hard heart was not something you had wanted for yourself. So this makes you conscious of your final spiritual homework - protecting your compassion from the temperament of the world, the "Sansar".

The spiritual gap in some of our relationships can assert itself so frequently that we don't want to bridge it anymore and start looking for options that can allow this gap to take its own time to narrow or even to stay the way it is. With just one simple making up of your mind, a relationship that used to feel like a heavy stone tied around the feet of someone who is trying to swim across a river, turns into a springboard for jumping into the next level of human incarnation. Your situation forces you into looking at it from somewhere else; it compels you into a paradigm shift. The moment you stand at a distance from the lawful unfolding of the karmic stuff in your incarnation, there is a silent explosion in your wisdom and the whole meaning of relationships undergoes a gigantic irreversible change. Thereafter, you are never able to relate with another, the way you used to. It is as if you have been taught by your disappointments to stop expecting the taste of oneness from those who are rooted in duality.

The presence of suffering in the lives of the ones you are concerned about, your, trying to do something about it, their being unable to comprehend your wisdom and the resultant helplessness regarding the whole situation leaves you with only one hope – to work on yourself and then design ways in which, what you know, can be shared with those who are ready for it and is available to the ones who are not. Readiness is like a door that has been opened for you to walk in whereas availability is like a knock on the door that is shut. The knock is barely audible and so mysterious that no one can hold you responsible for it. One such knock is your presence itself. The knowing is there, but there is no result oriented effort in it. There is no aggressive persuasion in it. It is as silent as the magnetizing of iron pins by a magnet or the conversion of carbon dioxide into oxygen by the chlorophyll in leaves.

The one who has attained renunciation is not afraid of relationships or relating but he never allows it to become a clinging of the mind. He has a great insight into the potential of ordinary relationships, to inflict suffering on the ones involved in them and therefore moves away from those that are unable to serve the purpose of a vehicle for mutual expansion. He can differentiate between spiritual oneness and temperamental duality and is determined not to allow his sacred space or the temple of his being to be invaded, exploited or emotionally blackmailed. The compassion in his heart is like a diamond in a safe; it is not something to be left unguarded and at the mercy of thieves and burglars. He knows that if he relates with the world from a space other than that of Bairag, he is very likely going to end up as a victim of the limitations of others and be pulled down from his realm of spiritual clarity into the agony of chaotic confusion. Therefore, he stays at a safe distance and even maintains it; for his own good and for the good of all.

The lack of innocence in the being of worldly men and women makes them incapable of establishing a bond, with the one who lives the truth. They are unable to realize that living truth cannot be sacrificed for the momentary pleasures of impermanent relationships and they want their cleverness to be entertained. But the Bairagi is not fascinated by emotional stuff that doesn't have truth at its core. He is too mature a soul for the games of love proposed by an impure heart and is more comfortable playing with innocent kids than conversing with egocentric adults. In the transparent eyes of a child, he gets a glimpse of the pristine self he sought as an ascetic and is mesmerized by it. He knows how rare and invaluable the quality is and what mankind has become because of the absence of it. He also knows that if he opens the gates of his being to the world and leaves the outcome of his interactions with the "Sansar" in the hands of those who consider themselves worldly wise, his bliss could easily be ruined by their ignorance and arrogance. Just as we don't allow everything and everyone into a beautiful and well looked after garden, the garden of consciousness has also to be protected from all those elements that can destroy its elegance. A discipline has to be followed; a code of conduct has to be adhered to. This is what we know as "Maryada" in the Indian religious texts. It is analogous to the safe distance that needs to be maintained on road between vehicles, in order to ensure a safe drive and manage all the traffic. This "Maryada" can prove to be a great discomfort for the ones who are used to invading, exploiting and interfering. The disobedient and the undisciplined perceive it as a barbed wire whereas the innocent perceive it as a sacred space. The wise respect it; the unwise despise it.

The Truth

I try to pull them out of their pain,
By making them aware of the ways of God;
But they are too proud to listen to me,
And find it very hard to consider me wise.

I am not trying to be wise I say,
I am just telling you the way it is;
And whether you listen to me or not,
That's the way it is - "It Is".

Truth is not a discussion to be had,
Truth is not an argument to be won;
Truth doesn't even require to be proved,
It just needs to be seen; Just seen.

For eyes that are innocent and curious enough,
And mind that is open to whatever can be;
Truth is like God's outstretched arms,

Surrounding you with the divine embrace.

For a heart that can sing with a bird on a branch,
And ears that can hear the whispers of intuition;
Truth is like a father holding his son,
Helping him walk across a busy road.

Truth is like the early morning breeze,
Silently moving across the town;
Sharing its freshness with those who have woken up,
And keeping it a secret for the ones asleep.

Truth is the knock on the door of your soul,
Asking it to join the dance of life;
Trying to free it from the prison of the mind,
And promising a liberty that knows no bound.

It is very important to understand that the Bairagi has not abandoned the world; he is simply not fascinated by it any more. Tired of all the pleasures and pains, the highs and lows, the ups and downs which ordinary life has to offer, he has taken refuge in a dimension that is stable. He has moved away from the variables and towards the constant. He has come home after wandering about for incarnations as a spiritual vagabond and has no desire to leave this space ever again. The "Sansar" cannot pull him anymore in directions that take him away from himself. His own odyssey is proof enough of all the meaningless endeavors designed by man to keep himself occupied and his own discoveries are authentic enough to enable him to say "No" to the persuasions of the less conscious. True renunciation is not like the painful quitting of an addiction; it is like the lack of interest in food after you have had a nice meal.

The Bairagi has spent a major part of his incarnation in simplifying things for himself and relationships are one of the most complex aspect of a human incarnation. They can often push you into dilemmas and become a test for your spirituality. They can make you stand at the edge of your rational mind with problems that can only be dissolved but never truly solved. They can wake you up to the parallel flow of individual incarnations and the cold perfection of the karmic law more successfully than anything else. They can leave you standing at a point where you feel utterly helpless and at the mercy of the discipline of the cosmos. Relationships can prove to be the toughest challenge for a soul that has become aware of its imprisonments and is working its way towards complete freedom and ultimate union. The Bairagi, after having lived these complexities for long enough, has arrived at the conclusion that attachment can do to the world he has created for himself, what poison can do to a food. He has to love the "Sansar" from a safe distance; a distance that can protect truth from the invasions of cleverness but can be bridged by sincerity.

The Ascetic

You cannot push through the gates of his heart,
And the harder you try, the faster they shut;
The games of love you have played all your life,
Are not the keys for unlocking his being.

The ascetic won't let you invade his space,
If aggression is all you have got to offer;
His heart is a garden for the children and the child like,
And there is no place for politics and power.

All that he wants from you is innocence,
So how could you say that he has asked for too much?
And if you can't even give him that,
What's the point in knocking on his door?

The kids have never been stopped for inquiry,
They move in and out of his space at will;
A three year old can make him run around,
Obeying the baby, as if it were a king.

This man surely doesn't belong to the world,
For the ways of the world are cunning and cruel;
Lost in the beauty of the truth he has tasted,
He lives a life very simple and straight.

•••••••••••••••••••••••••••••••

CHAPTER 4 - DYING WHILE ALIVE

There is a death that we all die and there is a death that only one in a billion volunteers for. The former, known as "Mrityu" in the Indian texts, can be witnessed everywhere as the departure of a soul from the body and the rituals that follow for the cremation or burial of that body. But the later, known as "Mahamrityu" or "The Great Death", is a spiritual experience which cannot be thus observed. It's the birth of a realization that takes place when a soul dis-identifies itself from the body, mind, senses and elements such as lust, anger and greed. Mrityu, in most of the cases, is as sudden as the strike of lightening whereas Mahamrityu is a conscious and deliberate witnessing of the destruction of that in us which is false - the destruction of illusion. In other words, Mahamrityu is the cremation of our false identifications.

Now, to be born as a soul, one has to die as a body, as a mind and as senses. It is as simple as that. Unless "this" dies; "That" cannot be born. Unless and until the nucleus of our being shifts from the ego to pure consciousness, the door which opens into the "Kingdom Of God" simply cannot be knocked. The death of the ego marks the birth of pure consciousness; the death of our identification with the body, mind and senses marks the birth of our identification with the soul. We come to know ourselves as an "Atman" only after having realized that we are none of the things we thought we were. We were never our body, we were never our mind and we were never our senses; it was all an error of judgment; it was all a result of wrong learning and false conditioning.

When I sat down for my first one hour meditation session, 23 years ago, I did not have the faintest idea that suffering is grace and the path that leads to bliss goes through the valley of spiritual death. Through these decades, there is something in me that has matured and ripened and I can now put all the pain, torment, confusion, despair, desolation and distress, to where it belongs. I can arrange all that chaos into a beautiful process of transformation and recognize the subtle shifts that were taking place in my inner world without my being aware of them. With every experience I went through, the gap between my perception of reality and the "Isness" of the existence was being bridged and veils which separated me from absolute truth were being lifted off one by one.

The wisdom of most of us remains an unrealized potential due to the denial of death and a desire to escape from suffering of all kinds. We imprison ourselves behind the four walls of our comfort zone and desperately try to ignore, both the presence of suffering in and around us and also the reality surrounding death. Suffering, for us, is something to be eliminated and death, something to be postponed. To some extent, suffering gets eliminated and death gets postponed. But this attitude of ours defines our limits and keeps us deprived of all the treasures that can only be assessed by embracing life in all its fierceness and beauty. The inclusion of death and suffering in all its forms into our perception of reality prepares our consciousness for change which is essential to maintain the flow of life and if we don't do so, each and every change, in and around us, appears to be threatening our very existence and consciously or subconsciously we try to resist it. Because of this resistance, the suffering that could have become our wisdom ends up becoming pain, helplessness, fear and doubt.

For example, aging, the evening of human incarnation, is perceived by most of us as a liability for the whole social setup and a flickering of the flame of life. The wisdom that could have bloomed by becoming aware of that which is timeless remains untouched by everyone because of the tendency of the mind to hold on to that which is subject to change. We invest so much of ourselves in the sand dunes of existence, up to and including our body that the formless at the nucleus of form totally misses our attention. That, which in an old person is as fresh as dew, gets buried under or contaminated by, the dust of denial. So much of conscious energy is wasted on feeling afraid and helpless that there is hardly anything left for reaching out to the soul. The Atman always finds us unavailable and completely lost in our despair. Like an angel standing next to us, unseen and unobserved, it patiently waits for us to free ourselves from our self imposed restrictions. The door to bliss is right in front of us but we choose to be misled by thought.

The glory of a human incarnation is in the fact that it provides us with an opportunity to liberate ourselves from the clutches of mortality. Right in the middle of an incarnation, one can wake up to see the amount of impermanence that is woven into the world of form. Our bodies are changing, our minds are changing, the social setup is changing, the social scenario is changing, the perception of people regarding the cosmos is changing, the means of living and communicating are changing, loved ones are dying and getting reincarnated, loved ones are taking birth and growing up – wherever you look, you see the signs of impermanence; whatever you touch seems to exist in time. The first time you become fully aware of the perishable nature of the world you are living in, it can pull you down into a very deep depression and leave you wondering what to invest yourself in. The difference between what it all is and what it appears to be is so seductive that the mind is unable to hold on to purpose as well as direction. Every person, in search of the truth, has to live with this confusion for quite some time and patiently wait for the mud of illusion to settle down and create space for clarity.

Our love for the comfort zone and our attachment to loved ones, beliefs and objects, robs us of our potential to realize the absolute truth. While spending and planning our incarnation, we try to exclude suffering and death and stay close to the pleasures which either make our senses feel alive or help us go to sleep. The more intense is our suffering, the more intense are our pleasures and intoxications. We do not allow our pain to get transformed into insight. We do not allow our death to introduce us to immortality. We do not allow our crucifixion to bloom into eternal love. The practice of dying while alive is, in a way, embracing the cross of our destiny and dropping down all the defenses which keep us safe and secure but cut us off from the parent source. The vulnerability of the human heart can lead us to the core of compassion if we do not guard and protect it from the presence of suffering and death.

When we look at life from within the ego we are guaranteed to get trapped in the personalizing of our incarnation. The giant mechanics which govern the flow of happenings are bound to become oblivious to the defense designed by the ego for its own survival. In order to preserve our separate uniqueness, we could be closing ourselves to the presence of all the truth that is destined to destroy our assumed identity. The collapsing of this house of cards is the inevitable change which every ascetic has to consciously go through for becoming available to the illumination of the Atman. The desperation involved in trying to hold on to security and certainty in a universe where everything is prone to change has to be consciously sacrificed for the sake of a greater realization.

It's very important to realize that the ego and the mind are the greatest barriers in the way of coming to know one's true self. Our thoughts and our virtual identity cut us off from the consciousness of the presence of the anchor of God. In the act of personalizing our incarnation, we get sucked into the thickness of illusion and our awareness of the total field in which we live is lost. The mind and the ego separate us from the Atman with a thick invisible wall of illusion and we go on living in darkness in spite of containing a door to illumination. The door is right in front of us but our occupation with the past and future, created for us by the mind, never allows us to knock it for long enough. The intense nature of our personality robs us of the opportunity to consciously experience the point of contact between the individual soul and the universal intelligence.

Now, when an individual soul longs for a total liberty from all the cages it experiences, the universal intelligence answers this prayer by designing opportunities or life situations that have got an inherent potential to destroy the boundaries of illusion. But being unable to recognize these, "Blessings in disguise", we are caught unaware by the intensity of our pain and fail to co-operate with God. We start resisting the change and we start defending our ego. We fall prey to the conflict between our desire to be free and our resistance to change. This battle of contradiction is the last nightmare of an ascetic and can go on for years or decades depending upon the strength of the desire and the magnitude of the clinging. At this stage, there is surely a lack of spiritual clarity and a resultant confusion, which can only be handled through a deepening of the wisdom and an expansion of the consciousness.

The events and circumstances of our life may have a big meaning for us but for the intelligence which has designed it all, they are just another something. Our profits and losses, our ups and downs, our victories and defeats, our fames and shames are nothing more than waves and ripples for this vast ocean of the mystery called life. The desire of an individual soul to go beyond being a puppet in the hands of the laws of the cosmos is just another wish for God to be fulfilled, another hunger to be satisfied, another thirst to be quenched. But it happens according to a design and suffering is an essential part of the same. This is what most of us fail to see; this is what most of us fail to understand. This is the major cause of all the restlessness and lack of faith amongst the ones seeking salvation.

The question is, "How will you deal with the presence of misery and death in your personal universe? Will you protect your heart from a burnout through escape and denial? Will you allow your comfort zone to make you cold and selfish? Will you divide this mankind into us and them for convenience? How do you draw the line between your limitations as a human being and your role as an instrument of compassion? How do you hold on to purpose and direction with all this unbearable pain in your incarnation? How do you heal the cosmos with a heart that has endured superhuman agony? Some fine day you will come to realize that you cannot afford your boundaries anymore and the separation between you and the cosmos has to be surrendered in order to bear the truth. Some fine day you will come to realize that the mind and the ego are incapable of bearing the unbearable and some other way of being has to be adopted to support your level of expression and interaction with the rest of the mankind.

In one of his talks on keeping the heart open in hell, Shri Ram Dass says, "Your bearing the unbearable; that is the root of the deepest compassion in the world." "Its' a fierce lesson", he says, "When you are being turned into an instrument of compassion." Most of us have had an experience of this fire of purification in one way or the other and know how our self oriented motives are sacrificed for the sake of a greater good. The magnificence of the game of life has little concern for our tiny egos and the ocean of universal intelligence cannot be manipulated by the molecule of our mind. Though the part we play in the unfolding of the whole is highly significant but that significance must not be overestimated. The ways of God cannot be judged by man and no matter how many rules we break, we cannot throw the parent source of this existence out of balance. When we become aware of our ignorance and start living at a level where the ego as a nucleus is not functional any more - that is the beginning of the blooming of our soul.

The flux of events in our life can sometimes be so overwhelming that it is hard to hold on to anything for the steering of the incarnation. The nature of the forces we are dealing with can be so complicated and deceptive that it becomes impossible to identify with our separated self and then make the right decisions. In order to know the flux, you may have to become the flux itself. You may have to reduce yourself to a mere channel for the flow of the living spirit in order to become acquainted with its way. As the banks are swept away by a river in flood, our individuality could be swept away by the powerful tides of truth. At some stage in our evolution, the ego is unable to contain what we know and the mind is unable to dominate the heart. From this point onwards, intuition serves as our guide and compassion becomes our residence.

When you have fully included death and suffering in your consciousness of the total field, the meaning of even something as insignificant as the brushing of your teeth is going to change. You will take care of them because they help you in chewing the food that nourishes the temple in which you live. The utility of the body as a vehicle for the incarnation of your soul will become very clear and obvious and you will see taking care of it as a responsibility rather than a worshiping of the self. You will decide to give up all such habits which are detrimental to the wellbeing of your physical self, not out of a lust for life, but to be able to perform better, on the stage of human incarnation. You would like to be healthy, not for indulging in the pleasures of the senses, but to be able to serve in a better way the ones in need of your talents and abilities. You would like to be healthy not because you are terrified of death, but because there are things you can do for others while in this human form and there are ways in which you can serve the lord while residing in this temple.

As a vehicle, the body, mind and senses are miraculous tools and if you know how to use them for your own expansion and the wellbeing of others, you will discover that you could not have wished for a better equipment to deal with the intricacies of a human incarnation. It is when you start dancing to their tunes, that these beautiful tools become ugly. The practice of dying while alive is, basically, dying to the irresistible temptations proposed by the pleasure seeking instincts of all the components other than pure consciousness. The incessant stream of thoughts and the non-stop internal dialogue has to be offered to the fire of awareness. The unending demands of the hungry senses have to be sacrificed at the altar of the bliss which does not belong to this world. "Chaitanya", the seat of the witness has to be declared as the master of the soul and everything else has to be taught to work in harmony with the wisdom of, what Shri Ram Dass calls, "The Intuitive Heart".

Before the senses and the mind declare this body dead and incapable of responding to the various stimuli, one should rise above the control they exercise on the pilot of the soul - the witness; the awareness or the consciousness. Thoughts and emotions should be considered as ripples produced by the throwing of a stone of some situation into the clear placid lake of our being. The gap between the stimulus and response should be mastered and conquered and none of our actions should ride the wild stallion of temperamental impulse. Our actions should pour out of an alertness, which is conscious of all the planes of reality simultaneously and not some unwise impulse, heavily affected by the intense nature of a relative truth. Our actions should be free of both the clinging of the mind and the shortcomings of a personality. They should point towards a dimension of our being deeply rooted in the vastness of the cosmos.

We must realize while residing in this body and being surrounded by all the comforts and securities, that other than the soul, there is nothing in our personal universe which really belongs to us. As soon as we leave this body and get migrated to another realm, all our possessions, all our property belongs to someone else. The house we used to live in has no place for us as a soul and if we still insist on hovering around, it is going to scare our loved ones. On that last journey after death the only luggage we can take along is our consciousness and deeds. We cannot take with us even a grain of sand from this world. So why not renounce all clinging to that which can never be really owned by us? Why wait for the lord of death to snap all our chords of attachment and tell us to leave this planet with nothing but a soul. Why wait for this world to cremate us and then get back to routine within a few days, reducing our existence to nothing but a love in the heart of a few faithful ones and memories in the minds of a few more.

We Forget

How easily we forget that we are guests on this land and some day shall have to pack up for where we have come from.

How much we get entangled in the solid dreams of the world, spending all our strength on achieving this or that.

How long it takes for us to realize the true nature of this life, the certain death which comes with birth and that which never dies. How soon we revert to our habits and routines when a loved one passes away; we act as if it is always going to be someone else's pyre.

How deep our desires are rooted in things far away from truth and compassion; we throw away the greatest gifts there are for worthless wants and pride.
How strong is our desire to keep on living, how desperate our denial of the truth; we can hear the footsteps of the inevitable approaching, but choose to ignore our intuition.

How unreasonable we become in dealing with this issue and are never prepared to die; we keep on investing our hope in this world and prefer to believe in a lie.
We allow ourselves to be guided by the treacherous patterns of illusion and offer our sacred innocence at the feet of greed and wrath.

We can refuse to belong to this world while we are living in it by pulling ourselves out of the mud of temptations and desires. We can become the one who is, "In this world but not of this world". It is definitely possible to uproot the soul from the soil of thoughts, emotions and sensuality and help it be seated, on the throne which cannot be usurped. While living on this planet, we can enter the realm which exists beyond the circumference of birth and death. The immortal part of our being can be known by consciously moving away from all that exists in time and space. Simply by the inclusion of suffering and death in our consciousness and a deliberate effort to rise above the clutches of our mind, we can become available to the mystery which waits for a soul that has liberated itself of all its' clinging. Instead of being a terror, the presence of suffering and death in our life can provide us with a spiritual breakthrough if totally accepted and embraced.

The "Big" life that we all want for ourselves is something which can only be manifested by dying to the virtual self. The ego cannot invite anything vast other than chaos and destruction. A drop of water cannot invite an ocean. But a drop of water can surely lose itself into the ocean by sacrificing its boundaries. Now, our identification with this boundary is so strong that we feel as if in the sacrifice of it our very existence will be sacrificed. The truth is that all that is lost in this process is nothing but a way of being. What used to walk around in the world as an ego, starts walking around as an awareness. An illusion gets destroyed, once and for all and a space gets created for new dimensions of reality. The individual personality, with sharp edges of pride and prejudice, is replaced by an environment of understanding and compassion which automatically liberates everyone who comes in touch with it. The canvas of our being expands in order to include the bigger picture in it. In opening up to all the different planes of reality we become available to the magnificence of life.

This magnificence of life cannot be lived by the ego. You cannot build a castle in a 100 sq. ft. plot of land. The various dimensions of reality, the various planes of reality, can only be experienced by someone who is open to all of them - someone who is not clinging to any fixed model of the way things are. A fixed model or a rigid belief is like a solid substance; it cannot flow. To experience flow, a liquidity is needed. Ego is solid; awareness is liquid. When you identify with awareness or consciousness, you are not threatened by change; you do not feel swept off your feet by the powerful currents of circumstances and in this absence of fear, you open up to the mystery which includes all forms of suffering and death. In this trusting of the divine flux, the purpose of all the change and transformation is revealed to you through strange unfoldings.

The patterns that cannot be seen by the naked eye or understood by the thinking mind are disclosed to the single eyed witness.

Now, the change involved in maintaining the cycles of life can sometimes be so powerful for our attachment that the mystery of it all gets lost in the emotional turmoil of despair. If we have not developed an understanding for the fierceness of the divine perfection, we cannot perceive the dance of life as a dance; the "Leela" as a "Leela". We have to have a space inside our being from where the clarity of vision can be restored; a dimension that has got the inherent potential to stay calm during all the cyclones of situations and circumstances. The ego and the mind are both not fit for this job. The ego tends to personalize everything and the mind tends to explain, that which it does not know, in terms of that which it knows. The song of truth can only be heard by the ears of pure consciousness. Neither the ego can hear it nor can the mind. They can surely analyze what has been heard by the consciousness but they cannot hear it. This song is beyond the grasp of personality and thought. Only when you are able to stand at a distance from both of them, does it become audible. And in this distancing, is their death. In your separation from them, they cease to exist.

In the act of liberating itself from all its imprisonments, the soul takes two major leaps. The first is from the ego and the mind into the consciousness; the second is from the consciousness into the super-consciousness. So the process of dying while alive is not abrupt; it is very natural and gradual. It occurs at a pace which can be handled by us. From individuality and thought, we first become the experience and then from the "Experiencer", we move on to become just the experience. The solid self first becomes a liquid one and then the liquid self becomes a vapor. From "My Body" and "My Mind", we move on to become "My Consciousness" and then from "My Consciousness", we move on to become "The Consciousness". Spiritual death is not like the death of someone in an accident; it is like the death of someone from a life threatening disease - you are fully aware of the collapsing of what you thought you were. You are fully aware of the demolition of your personal universe. A world of illusions is destroyed right before your eyes and there is nothing you can do other than allow it to be so. The very nature of your predicament leaves you with no other option but to watch as if it were happening to someone else.

But it is this helpless witnessing, which finally introduces you to the wisdom of the universe and defines very clearly, the purpose of your incarnation. The mystery of an incarnation cannot be understood without surrendering to it. It will not reveal itself to someone who is making frantic efforts to rescue himself or others from the clutches of suffering and death. It will manifest in a consciousness that has included both of them and has merged with the greater mechanics of life. As long as you are pushing any part of life away from you, your wisdom will not be able to bloom and you won't be able to see how the beginnings and ends all go into the making of a life that is immortal. When the surrender is complete, the purpose of our incarnation shows up from behind the curtains of attachment.

There is a play between polarities, between good and evil, between male and female, between right and wrong, between, what the Chinese call, Yin and Yang, which cannot be seen without dying to the ego. It is visible only to those who have managed to pull themselves out of everything that has got duality at its core. These mysterious equations become known only to the one who can resist the temptation of trying to balance them. In dying to the equation, the equation gets balanced. In surrendering yourself to the wisdom of the cosmos, the wisdom is revealed. That dimension in us, which has got the potential to rise above all the situations and circumstances, can only be accessed through a natural renunciation of the elements which encourage duality. And the soul firmly rooted in the experience of "One" can clearly see the unfolding and blooming of all the various forms around it.

The first major realization that one experiences after dying to the virtual self, is the stages of human evolution being exhibited by the behavior of individual souls. The puzzling nature of your interactions, with people located at a unique point on the graph of spiritual growth, gets simplified through your understanding of the various levels of consciousness or awareness. You are able to see how the quality of your relationships is decided by the amount of awareness and the amount of commitment to truth. You are able to see how the presence of suffering and death fits into the fabric of life. And when you start living with this realization inside, it creates a spiritual environment that can liberate everyone it touches. The individual differences become less threatening, for the peace and harmony of the getting together of souls and the uniqueness of everyone involved, doesn't feel the need to sacrifice itself, in order to keep the spirit of togetherness alive.

Another major paradigm shift that occurs in your perception of the universe is that the power of variables beyond your control becomes very obvious to you. The force of everyone's destiny, including yours, expresses itself so strongly that you see no point in trying to manipulate the unfolding of the cosmos. You start resting in a space that provides a very clear view of all the basic patterns of life. There is a clarity in your thought and an elegance in your expression which could not have been possible as long as you were imprisoned by the body, mind and senses; as long as you were fiercely trying to protect your uniqueness. You start identifying with a vastness in which phenomenon appear and disappear, an element that is enriched by each and every experience, but does not try to hold on to any of them.

With the death of the ego, the soul becomes capable of comprehending the intelligence of God to a much greater extent. All the energy that was being wasted, on defending the virtual boundaries, becomes available to the soul for reaching out to the one behind the many. All the consciousness that was trapped in the karmic stuff of the incarnation is released through an understanding of the basic structure of life.

The Transition

The leaves of the trees seemed greener and brighter,
The blue of the sky more beautiful and serene;
The chirping of the birds and the innocent talks of children,
All seemed to make a sense it had never made before.

Something had happened to me along the way,
But the subtlety of it made this hard to explain;
My seeking and my suffering had given birth to a mystery,
And hereafter I knew, things would never be the same.

The messages from another world were clear and precise,
There was someone taking care of me, all day, all night;
I felt like a child with a father nearby,
He guide me, he scolded me but never left me alone.

That there was a life like this, I had only learnt from books,
A power just one thought away, was beyond all measures and limits;
The way it moved the pieces around left no doubt in my mind,
That the entire universe was at its command and time was a play for it.

I walked around like a foreigner in this world,
Acutely aware of the patterns that exist;
The purpose of my life had revealed itself,
A curtain had been lifted off my views and perceptions.

I could see the river of life flowing through me,
The current too strong for me to resist;
My wisdom was in surfing the waves of events,
And listening to the silent instructions of God.

The words of all the sacred books became as fresh as dew,
The bliss they promised, the insights they offered were beyond the
dimensions of time;
The nectar of truth had travelled through the centuries to quench my
spiritual thirst,

I knew what the sages wanted to say but couldn't express through script.

The silence of this cosmos was not a silence for me anymore,
I knew the power it contained and the language of laws it spoke;
I could see that the world we so admire is just the tip of an iceberg,
And there are nine more parts to be discovered by those who live the truth.

When I wake up in the morning and look up at the stars,
The vastness of the sky makes my mind expand;
The sparks of light and the black background,
Help me to touch my own emptiness.

The ideas that originate after a cup of green tea,
The thoughts which come together to direct my life;
The beautiful explosions that occur in my silence,
Are all a gift of God for me.

The hunger and the flavors of food being cooked,
The hundreds of seeds, roots and fruits we can eat;
The conversion of it all into bones, flesh and blood,
What greater miracle do we all wish to see?

There is nothing ordinary in the life that we live,
Every speck of it contains a thousand secrets;
A simple event when passed through the prism of wisdom,
Breaks up into a spectrum of insights and wonders.

The ability of the eyes to see, the ears to hear and the tongue to taste,
The way we are able to distinguish between a smell and a fragrance;
The touch, the feelings, the senses, the mind and all the magic we have
taken for granted,
Really needs to be looked at again with the curiosity of a child.

I often find myself looking at the flames of a fire,
Wondering about their power and potential;
You can throw into them anything you feel like,
And most of it will be reduced to an ash.

The simple sleep that we just slide into after a hard day's toil,
Could be a subject for years of study if the mystery in it were to be known;
Just think about the way it creates for us a rest as essential as breath,
The dreams it designs with the excess of thoughts, the peace it provides
every night.

The sparrows, crows, parrots, pigeons and cranes flying all over the sky,
Make me aware of the part I play in the overall scheme of things;
I can see one God, scattered all around, in all these different forms,
Without the disguise this game I suppose would have lost its element of
surprise.

The early morning breeze, the sunlight, the rain, the freely showered
bounties of God,
The love I receive from twenty different directions and all of it
unconditional;
The powers that protect me from dangers everyday and guide me with
sound advice,
What greater wealth could I seek for myself? What better world could I
pray for?

The smile on the face of a happy child, the blooming of these flowers of
innocence,
The hungry being fed, the hurt being healed, the hearts where compassion
can be found;
There's so much on this earth to be adored and admired if only we could
see as it is,
I pray therefore for a vision that is clear, a heart that is pure and a soul that
is clean.

●●●●●●●●●●●●●●●●●●●●●●●●●●●●●●

"Be honest in your practice and be generously critical in analyzing your progress."

CHAPTER 5 - METHODS I USED TO KNOW MYSELF

(i) **Mantra.**
(ii) **Reading Sacred texts.**
(iii) **Satsang.**
(iv) **Guru Kripa.**
(v) **Listening.**
(vi) **Relationships.**
(vii) **Breathing.**
(viii) **Music.**
(ix) **Food.**

If you spend some time briefly studying the doctrines of the major religions of the world e.g. Buddhism, Jainism, Hinduism, Islam, Christianity and Sikhism, you will notice that there are innumerable methods and techniques for exploring the depths of this existence and for finding out who we are. You can take any route which suits you, depending upon where you are, but at the end of your journey you will be surprised to discover that you could have reached your destination from any direction; it would have made little difference. Every religious sect is a route to God and no one is better or worse than the other. With sincerity, persistence and faith, you can become one with God through the practice of any one of them.

The techniques we find most appealing, for moving into the depths of our being, have a lot to do with our past as a soul. We are inclined to make a speedy progress, in an area of learning that is familiar to us, based upon our previous incarnations. It is easier to slide in the grooves created by our practice in the past and this is precisely what enables our intuition to choose a spiritual method from the wide range of options available. Our current incarnation is nothing but a continuity of a long process of evolution in all the various dimensions which constitute our being. We have been on this planet, innumerable times before and all that we have learnt so far has become a part of our consciousness.

In the last two and a half decades, I have studied and practiced many techniques, to evolve as a consciousness and they have all gone into the making of whatever I am, but I shall discuss only the ones that have contributed the most to my spiritual growth and have been a part of my daily routine during some of the highly challenging years of this particular incarnation. I think the success of any method, as a vehicle for transformation, depends to a great extent, upon the intelligence and attitude of the practitioner. The method in itself is merely a potential; it is the sincerity and dedication of the practitioner which provides it with flesh and bones and pumps life into it. If ten people are given a Mantra and asked to report back after a year, they will not have made equal gains from the use of it as a technique. So, a method must not be held responsible for a lack of enthusiasm in your approach and should be used the way a beginner uses water in learning how to swim. Be honest in your practice and be generously critical in analyzing your progress. With the help of your intellect and intuition you will certainly succeed in making your spiritual dreams come true and the bliss which will thus manifest will be beyond all your expectations.

i – Mantra

I do not remember when I was introduced to a Mantra as a child but as a grown up, it was in the year 2005 that I received it from an enlightened being, Sant Harbhajan Singh Ji. He whispered it very religiously, three times in each ear and instructed me to recite it as if I was talking to God. Since then, it has been my major spiritual practice and the backbone of my routine. Most of my days begin with a one and a half hour of reciting the name of God which in my case is "Waheguru". During the day also, every time I am reminded of it by my identity as a man of the path, I start reciting it softly until something else grabs my attention. So, in a way, it has become the background music of my life. And if someone were to ask me what is it that I have gained from all these twelve years of practice, I think it is, "Insights". I haven't practiced hard enough to be able to fly with the Mantra but I have surely succeeded in pulling myself out of a lot of subtle stuff. The beautiful fruits of knowing that the name of God has born, have introduced me to a taste that cannot be experienced with the senses. By silently working on the deepest levels of the clinging of my mind, the name of god has liberated my soul of a thousand mysterious bondages.

Every time I recite the name of God, it serves the purpose of creating a context in which to look at my own incarnation and all the rest of the universe. I am reminded of so many facts that we all can easily forget while dealing with the details of our life on this particular plane of existence. It reminds me of the one behind the many, the dance of life and the mysterious blending of formless with form. It pulls me out of the gravity of situations and circumstances and encourages me to look at everything as if it were nothing but a passing show. The purpose and meaning of my incarnation becomes much more defined by the clarity of vision I gain from tuning in to the almighty.

Now, if I were to explain the significance of a Mantra to a scientist, the only way I could do it would be by speaking in terms of frequency. The vibrations created from the repetition of the name of God are in tune with the frequency of the formless behind all form. So, in a way, we are using the medium of sound as a vehicle to come to God. We are trying to establish a resonance between the unseen part of our being and the source of all creation. It is no coincidence that the first experience of having established yourself in the dimension of pure consciousness is that of light and sound. It is so because that is the fundamental characteristic of the source of all manifestation.

In terms of its efficiency as a Yogic (Spiritual) method, Mantra's success comes from its ability to reduce our incessant thinking to one single thought - the thought of God. The job of the mind during your reciting is merely that of putting the alphabets of the word together. So, in a way, you are using the mind to go beyond the mind. The very nature of our mind is such that it needs some mental task to perform. So that need can be fulfilled by asking the mind to keep the Mantra going and in this resting or relaxing of its agitation, our energy becomes available to us to be channeled towards consciousness. If in addition to the repetition of a word, we also use the beads or "Mala" it further assists us in moving within by taking care of the agitation of the body and also synchronizing the beads with the breath, thus aligning all the elements of our being.

I have noticed a very prominent difference between the quality of days I begin with 90 minutes of reciting the Mantra and those that I don't. They seem to be belonging to two completely different mediums; as if one were air and the other were water. When I have practiced in the morning, there is something in me that seems to have opened up to some higher realms of existence and I am able to take a generous view of the details of my incarnation. When I miss my early morning practice, I am highly prone to getting sucked into the negativity I am surrounded by and my perception is afflicted by the patterns of mass consciousness. My mind is narrowed and my concerns are exaggerated. I forget what the game of life is all about and become overly anxious about trivial matters. I lose my perspective and offer the reigns of my emotional state into the hands of fear and doubt.

In the sacred text of the Sikhs, almost once on each and every one of the 1430 pages, the significance of the reciting of the Mantra has been clearly emphasized. An equal emphasis is on the role of the Guru in pulling us out of the marsh of karma. Since I read about 30 pages of the text almost every day, I am reminded every time of how important it is for me to be committed to my religious practice. "In no form other than the human one can a soul recite the name of God", the text says "And if you fall down into an animal form you may have to wait for thousands or may be millions of years to get another chance to do so", it adds. Since no one can question even an alphabet of what the enlightened beings have to say, Mantra is surely on the top of the list of methods I rely upon for helping me sail across the ocean of life.

It is also mentioned in the sacred texts that the name of god and ego cannot coexist in one body. So, in a way, God's name is the ideal medicine for the ailment called ego. Drop by drop the Mantra falls upon the rock of ignorance and wears away its solid boundaries based on duality. The name of God pulls us away from self oriented motives, encourages the spiritual heart to be generous and guides the mind to think in terms of compassion. Ego feeds upon the concept of a separated self while the name of God points towards the "One" in the form of "Many". Ego has got a "Me" at its nucleus while the name of God has got "Us" in it. Ego claims to be the "Doer" while the name of God reminds us that we are merely instruments through which the divine plan unfolds.

Another very powerful aspect of the use of Mantra as a spiritual practice is that even the most uneducated man on earth can comfortably recite it and evolve. Even a simple peasant, who has never been to a school, can reap all the spiritual benefits by diving into the depths of the name of God. There are no complicated Shlokas to be remembered, no sophisticated rituals to be performed; there is neither any intellectual table tennis nor any breathing technique to be mastered - it's all simplified into a single word which is to be uttered with love. What more could you expect from the enlightened ones? What better route to the self there could be?

"In no form other than the human one, can a soul recite the name of God"

ii - Reading Sacred Texts

The wisdom of the ones who became one with God would have definitely remained unshared, if it had not been passed on to all of us in the form of words and signs. We would all have lived on islands of experience with no common source of inspiration and guidance to look up to or refer to. Without these spiritual maps, it would have been much more tough to discover the treasure within and to make some meaning out of all the chaos and anarchy we are surrounded by. The words contained by religious books are certainly instrumental in bridging the gap between the ones who came to realize the truth and the ones who wish to realize it. Without these seeds, the tree of knowledge could not have spread itself or passed on its essence. It would have lived and died in time and ceased to exist thereafter in any way or form.

When you read words written by the enlightened ones, you are automatically pulled in the direction of enlightenment. Our soul is nourished by the wisdom that is intricately woven in the form of these "Sutras" and the taste of what the wise ones had experienced is passed on to us in a mysterious way. These beings were firmly rooted in the dimension of pure consciousness and their expression could not be polluted by the temptations of the world. They really knew what true freedom is and were not talking about glimpses of liberty. They had transcended the vulnerability of the soul which has not yet freed itself of the body, mind and senses. So, what they had to say was coming from a state of being that has got an unwavering compassion at its core. And there is something in us which is as sacred as these Saints. It is this very element of ours that is encouraged by their words and is touched by their message.

Now, I usually read about 30 pages from these ancient treasure houses of wisdom and the texts I read from are principally the "Adi Granth" and the "Dasam Granth". It roughly takes 1 and a ½ hour to do so and by the end of these 90 minutes, I get a very strong feeling of something inside me having made a prominent shift. Most probably, it is perspective. It is as if I have just had an aerial view of the world I live in, as if everything in my life, including my body, mind and senses have been redefined for me so that I may not forget what this game is all about. For ninety minutes, I look at life through the eyes of these realized beings and that vision stays with me for the rest of the day. These daily encounters of mine with truth, gradually pull me out of the attachment I have for all that is going to change and introduce me to a grand view of my own incarnation which I could not have had from within my limitations.

It is absolutely certified that the element of our being which is fed and encouraged becomes stronger than the rest of them and ultimately starts affecting all our actions and motivations. If it is greed, our whole way of living becomes an expression of greed. If it is anger, we end up living in an angry world. By the same principle, if we feed and encourage pure consciousness, it gradually illumines all the dark and ignored corners of our being. Reading sacred text is one way of feeding our consciousness with truth, wisdom, oneness and compassion. It can surely prove to be one of the healthiest diets for maintaining the health of our soul. The lower elements are still there, but they are not strong enough to dominate. They are now in tune with the motives of your knowing, like the strings of a finely tuned instrument.

For something as subtle as the consciousness, we need subtle diets such as - words of wisdom and without this shift from the gross to the subtle, nothing significant is possible, in the direction of knowing who we truly are. You have to move within, quite far from the body in order to discover the wonders of the mysterious world which exists between the formless and the form. All the words in the Holy Scriptures came from beings who existed on the cusp between the world of form and the formless God. So, when you read from them, your soul is nourished with the mystery that surrounds this phase of transition. You get a very strong feeling of what it is like to be "In this world but not of this world". These words remind us again and again that it is possible to transcend all our self imposed limitations and live a life which is not threatened by suffering, change and death. The taste of the point where exactly a human being comes in contact with God, is really very helpful, in encouraging the consciousness to pull itself away from its identification with the body, mind and senses. It is this taste that makes it move towards the higher realms.

I personally feel that there has been a great deal of misunderstanding regarding the meaning of all the religious texts in relation to the life of an individual. We must realize that these treasures are not just to be worshipped; they are to be read and understood and then incorporated in our everyday life. They are a guidance from the messengers of God on how to steer our incarnation in the direction of bliss and liberty and unless we practice the ideals preached by all the wise ones, nothing is going to change in the way we live and die. The instructions provided therein are absolutely simple and clear and anyone with an open mind can hear the message aloud. It is, I think, in the act of protecting his rationalizations that man becomes unavailable to truth and the beauty of the truth contained in these texts is that it is an absolute one. It is not relative. It is not susceptible to change because of an incomplete knowing. It is eternal and about that in us which does not exist in time.

The success of written words in being absorbed by our soul lies in the fact that there is no personality which could prove to be difficult for our basic nature. All that there is, is the essence of a knowing which vibrated with life centuries ago. Most of us are uncomfortable with taking teachings from a living master. But if the same teaching is offered to us in the form of written word, it is easier for our ego to digest the truth that has got the potential to destroy a false structure of beliefs. Written word does not have a temperament and therefore allows us to learn from it at our own natural pace. A living master can change his tone if he is irritated by our arrogance. He could even tell us to stay away from him for a while, work on ourselves and become palatable for his tolerance. But written words are much more liberal in the case of human imperfections and it is so because they do not have to suffer at the hands of our attitude.

Another factor responsible for the success of written word, as an instrument of learning, is the way it gets engraved on our mind. When you learn by heart the words of the sages and offer them some space in your conscious mind, from there they seep into the subconscious and like seeds hidden beneath the surface of the soil, start waiting for congenial circumstances to grow into plants of knowing. Spiritual teachers have always emphasized a lot on remembering as much of the Holy Scriptures as we comfortably can and then praying for the meaning of those words to reveal itself to our soul. These words, when allowed to become an integral part of our self can gradually start aligning all the molecules of our being so as to synchronize with the essence of the wisdom they contain. They start growing and maturing from inside out.

Although there is no ideal way of reading a sacred text but I personally find the study more fruitful when done with a mind at rest. Agitation of any kind is not good for this method to work. The more relaxed and receptive you are, the easier it is for the wisdom of the sages to be comprehended by your consciousness. The mind is not a reliable tool for relating with that which is not yet known. But it can surely be used very beautifully to organize and analyze our past experiences and then listen carefully to what the wise had to say about that which we have already gone through. When read from the seat of spiritual heart, with complete faith and trust, the words of our ancient mystics can suddenly become vibrant with a truth that never ages or dies. It is absolutely natural for this to happen since the basic structure or fabric of life has always been the same. The changes owing to scientific inventions cannot affect or alter the fundamental elements, which go into the making of the world we live in.

When read with a childlike innocence and curiosity, the sacred texts remind us that life is not what it appears to be. When that which lies to the left and right of our incarnation is included in our vision, the meaning and purpose of every little thing in our world undergoes a change. The Sages bring to our notice, all the ways in which man is inclined to waste his precious incarnation and advice us to be aware of the various baits of desires and temptations. Ordinary poetry doesn't do that. But the poetry in the books of truth was all written with the purpose of liberating man of his chains and for helping him see his own glory buried beneath the layers of illusion. The mystics were very careful with the words they chose to express themselves; it was always the most significant and nothing unnecessary. So, on one hand, our holy books introduce us to the most elegant use of language and script and on the other hand, they warn us of all the pitfalls of a human incarnation.

"The mystics were very careful with the words they chose to express themselves; it was always the most significant and nothing unnecessary."

iii – Satsang

As a plant needs protection from so many things to grow into a full-fledged tree, so does a man in search of meaning need protection from the insanity of the world. The chaos due to social unconsciousness can be really very challenging for the harmony which a compassionate soul has managed to create for itself with the help of all its knowing. In the community of men and women on the path of righteousness or what we call a "Satsang", an individual soul seeking salvation finds the spiritual and emotional security it needs. The conviction and faith of an individual, no matter how strong it is, can be often overwhelmed by the forces of ignorance. At such times, one longs for a system that can support it in every possible way. Thus, the greatest purpose of Satsang is to keep the spirit of truth alive in those whose life is a statement of "Dharma".

Being a social animal, man is not biologically supposed to live alone on an island. But then, how does he find the company which can bring out the best in him and help him rise above the pull of self-imposed restrictions? How does he have a family of well-meaning people to belong to? How does his fundamental need of relating with another get fulfilled? Where does his soul feel at ease and at home? The answer is – Satsang. In the togetherness of an enlightened master and his devotees and in the sharing of a common cause, all the emotional cravings of an individual soul automatically get gratified. The environment of compassion generated from a commitment to the core values of humanity serves as a powerful inspiration for every rational human being to be kind, sincere and generous.

The support provided by Satsang to a man or woman of truth is highly essential to avoid an emotional burnout. The magnitude of ignorance in the world we live in can deplete us to such an extent that if there were no community to heal our continuously breaking heart, we would soon run out of the strength to fight the weird battles of life. The forces we have to deal with, in the act of preserving our freedom, can be so complicating in their nature that they can easily throw our whole personal universe completely out of balance. It is the compass of Dharma or righteousness which helps us maintain our direction when everyone around us seems to have lost a rational approach. It's tough to be a man of truth, as most of you must have realized by now and without a spiritual brotherhood, we would definitely feel deserted and betrayed.

Now, the question is, "Exactly what kind of a gathering can be defined as a Satsang?" People get together to enjoy a live music concert. People get together to watch a movie in a theatre. They get together in sports stadiums to watch a game being played. They gather in large amounts on the occasion of wedding and birthday parties. But none of these gatherings has anything to do with a Satsang. As I have come to know it, Satsang is a get-together where truth can be shared without any fear. It is founded on the principle of a mutual consent that if someone wishes to speak, he has the liberty to speak the truth and the ones who are listening to him have got the guts to listen to the truth. It is an arrangement in which formalities have been cut down to the minimum and we are encouraged to be authentic and transparent. The purpose is absolutely clear - to help each other in living a conscious and meaningful life; i.e. assisting the human incarnation to be of maximum benefit to the soul. Satsang is a place where we are recognized as a soul and where all the emphasis is on teaching us, how to bloom as a spiritual being having a human experience.

It was around the year 2012 I think that I became acutely aware of the effect of the collective vibrations of a religious get-together on the state of my being. By then, I had practiced a lot of meditation techniques and spiritual methods and they had escorted me to the point where one is able to see that which cannot be seen. I had moved into the subtle world of frequencies and vibrations and the pool of environment which a Satsang had to offer was too strong and distinct for my consciousness to miss. The difference between oneness and duality, in the form of my interactions with fellow beings, had clearly stated itself and Satsang was a place I could count on for providing me with a real experience of unity. In the faith and selfless service of a community, I was able to see the possibility of a world where man is not crippled by his individual needs and desires.

The potential of a Satsang to liberate a soul of its confinements, lies in the fact, that when souls come together to meditate, pray and share the truth, the field thus generated is not an addition of their energies - it is exponential in nature. The difference it makes is not quantitative; it is qualitative. It is enriched by the inclusion of dimensions unknown to us in the ordinary world. The life we ordinarily live is very close to that of an animal. It revolves around our basic instincts and rarely exhibits true compassion. But in the presence and company of an enlightened one, our heart learns to open up and allow the pain and suffering of others to touch its vulnerability. This expansion of our being creates space for new dimensions which help us pull ourselves out of the loss and pain of our incarnation. And beyond all loss and pain, is the freedom that is known to very few.

In one of his talks, Shri Ram Dass states that the most meaningful relationships in our life are the ones in which there is a mutual understanding to be able to share the truth. The "Being able to do so", is in itself, enough to enrich the bond, he says. The capacity of truth to destroy prison walls and coax a consciousness into expansion is exactly where all its success as a spiritual path comes from. Satsang happens to be the ideal place to look for such relationships in which a fundamental commitment to truth has already been made. Here you won't feel the need to stay on guard for protecting yourself from the invasions and intrusions of treachery and deceit. You can comfortably relax and bathe in the security of a brotherhood that is destined not to let you down. Believe me; the company of souls which are basically good at heart can restore your ability to trust another human being. They can really save you from an emotional breakdown. Satsang is a refuge for the wounded compassion and the ailing heart.

As parched land craves for rain, every few weeks or so, I feel a very compelling urge to be in the company of my spiritual brotherhood. Though I am surrounded by an ocean of people but most of them are like the salty water which cannot quench a thirst. The gap between the way I see the world and their priorities is so great that nothing very gratifying can be expected to manifest out of our interactions. At the end of every interaction, I find myself learning to cope with a helplessness and hopelessness which I was destined to experience in the process of evolving. The spiritual climate in which a free exchange of thoughts and emotions is possible is missing in most of my relationships with people who are deeply rooted in their attachments. I feel highly confined by the limiting potential of all these peripheral acquaintances and long for the ones that can provide me with the experience of an inner expansion and the dissolving of my boundaries.

Satsang is not just an assurance for your belief system; it is a food for your love starved being. When you long for the company of your spiritual brotherhood, it does not imply that you are looking for a spiritual shelter which can justify your ideology. This pool of unconditional love and oneness is not for entertaining and encouraging our ailments; it is for introducing us to the taste of an absence of duality and a quality of being which comes into existence when we reside in pure consciousness. Satsang should be seen as the source of an experience that cannot be found anywhere else. Even the life of an enlightened being would surely become very dry and boring if there was no Satsang in it. It is in the sharing and expressing of it that love blooms as a blessing for the whole of mankind.

Whenever a yearning soul becomes one with God, the immediate next desire that pours out of its brimming is to create an arrangement which can make it possible for the bliss to be shared with those who are ready for it. The arrangement has to be such that it can accommodate the whole range of temperaments found in men and women. It has also to take into account, the children and the old. It has to have a discipline and it has to have a freedom. It has to be strong in its expression of the intention to wake everyone out of his spiritual slumber but without being harsh for the pace at which most of us learn and grow. Satsang is such an arrangement. It is an enlightened being's design for working as an instrument of knowing; for inviting ultimate freedom into the lives of the ones imprisoned by the mind. Satsang is the school where we learn how to live.

As a cloth is dyed by a dyer, I find my subtle body dyed by the collective vibrations of Satsang every time I join my brothers in faith with devotion in my heart. And then when I come back into the world, it starts fading out leaving me with only that which I have earned through my personal effort. But the experience of having tasted something of the beyond stays with me like a hangover. It keeps on steering, my incarnation in general and my spiritual practice in particular, in the right direction. It provides me with an idea of the blissfulness that is waiting for me on the far end of my journey. It enables me to contrast the ordinary desire driven life with a peaceful state of being and then move confidently through the chaos of conflicting viewpoints.

"Satsang is a place where we are recognized as a soul and where all the emphasis is on teaching us, how to bloom as a spiritual being having a human experience."

IV - Guru Kripa

After going through the 84 lakh incarnations and being born as a human being, with the whole of the cosmos before his eyes and a million paths to take, don't you think that the chances of man choosing the right one are quite bleak? Don't you think that without a higher power guiding him all the way, he could easily get lost in the jungle of options? Don't you think that if he leaves his incarnation on an auto pilot mode, he could never make it out of the vicious cycle of birth and death? I personally feel that the significance of a Guru cannot be under estimated. Just as a human baby cannot survive easily without a parent to take care of it, man cannot reach out to the light of salvation without the parental guidance of a master.

I truly consider myself blessed to be born in a family which is purely vegetarian and has accepted an enlightened being as its spiritual guide or mentor. So my birth, in itself, is Guru Kripa. I could have been born amongst people who did not have anything to do with truth. An Indian poet by the name of Pandit Hardiyal, has referred to seven major fruits of good karma and the family one is born into, happens to be at the top of his list; the other six being healthy body, good looks, material abundance, obedient children, good education and a harmonious marriage. My mother was a faithful housewife and my father an honest government employee. My grandfather was a real ascetic who got up at 1 a.m. every morning for his daily reciting of the Mantra. So, I had a good basic foundation to start with.

As a child I used to accompany my father on many of the religious get-togethers and got a chance every time to be blessed with the Guru's presence. Even without my being aware of it, I was being showered with bounties unknown to a worldly man. But it was at the age of 21 that I came into direct contact with my Guru and from here my whole incarnation was destined to take a quantum leap. Since then, all my years have been an effort to liberate myself from the clutches of spiritual slavery. In a way, the whole of my youth was dedicated to the attainment of knowing. But who told me to do so? That's Guru Kripa. You cannot prove it to anyone but it is written all over your destiny.

By the age of forty, I had become aware of the level at which the game between a real master and a disciple is played. Not only that, I was even becoming good at it. Because that was all in my life which fascinated me and made me feel alive, other than a few meaningful relationships. My relationship with my Guru provided my incarnation with almost all its purpose. If I failed here, all my worldly successes put together meant nothing and if I succeeded here, all my worldly failures meant nothing. The amount of truth in it and the number of dimensions it included made this single bond the most significant aspect of my life. My spiritual practice was now more oriented towards living up to the expectations that a master has from a disciple. The accumulation of knowledge was replaced by the sacrificing of it and in all my actions and interactions there was an acknowledging of the fact that I was being closely observed.

In the simplest terms, Guru Kripa can be defined as the magical way in which a liberated being tries to free someone from his visible and invisible imprisonments. If the imprisonment is that of poverty, he tries to make you rich. If it is sickness, he tries to restore you to health. If you are rich and healthy but spiritually enslaved, he tries to help you rise above your attachment with the body, mind and senses. So, on one hand, the Guru takes care of your immediate needs and on the other hand he assists in the blooming of the purpose of your incarnation. There is a balance in his approach regarding these two, equally significant realities and he tries to make it sure that one doesn't suffer at the hands of the other. Such balance cannot be found in the life of those who have invested too heavily in one dimension of reality or the other.

Not only does the Guru take care of your needs, wants, desires and ambitions, he also tries to protect you from an inevitable impending disaster. He even prepares you for it in advance. The ability of the Guru to see the past, present and future, both in the case of an individual and that of the whole of mankind, puts him in a very definite position to decide what is good for everyone in general and an individual in particular. When he tells you the way things are going to be, he is not doing so on the basis of some guesswork or statistical data, he is predicting through the power of his vision. But he is a visionary, not a palmist or astrologer. If there is something he thinks you better not know he will prepare you and take care of you accordingly, keeping the secret in his heart all through. In the end, it will all be for your good.

Now, what many of us are unable to comprehend is - grace in the form of suffering and loss. If a sick person becomes healthy again with the grace of the Guru, no one finds it difficult to see the obvious hand of the master in it. But if a healthy one falls sick due to some unknown karmic reasons, most of us find it hard to digest the truth that this is also Guru Kripa. In fact it is only in such fierce forms that grace takes off to a dimension of its own. When I look back at my own past I can see the various shades of it methodically working on the core of my being to set it free of all the deep rooted attachments and identifications. All my agony and despair seems to fit into a perfect planning designed by a power that knows no limits.

The best evidence to be found in the life of someone who has received the blessings of a Guru, is, spiritual growth and the blooming of compassion. Though material abundance can also be showered upon you in order to make you happy, but Guru Kripa should never be measured in terms of all these worldly benefits. If you happen to be one of his favorites, the Guru would naturally like to give you the best he has got; the jewels in his crown. And those jewels are - the jewels of wisdom and compassion. A wise and compassionate being is what the Guru would like you to become as a result of all your practice, as a result of your austerity. He would not like you to get trapped by spiritual materialism and the glamour of holiness. He would keep on silently working on the cultivation of the real thing in your heart. With his mysterious tools, he will keep on sculpturing your soul.

I can clearly see, from where I am this moment, that there was some heavy karmic stuff which I was supposed to deal with, in this incarnation and without the unconditional and invisible support of my master, I don't think I would have managed to do so in a wise and intelligent way. The unbearable cannot be born without the strength of absolute faith and such faith cannot be developed in the absence of true compassion. It was from the presence and guidance of my Guru that I derived such strength. It was the promising shade of his being which kept me going through the dark nights of my soul. The storms that I survived were powerful enough to sweep me off my feet if the roots of the love I shared with my master were not deep and strong enough. My own capacity to deal with all these challenges was certainly not adequate.

Satguru Jagjit Singh Ji used to say that the devotee is like a cube of ice and the Sansar or world is like an ocean of fire; if the cube does not melt, it is because of Guru Kripa. A good example of the kind of protection that a devotee receives from his master is the incident of a 17th century sikh, known by the name of Bhai Biddi Chand. During one of his brave exploits, when he needed a place to hide from the Mughals who were trying to capture him, he was compelled by the gravity of the circumstances to hide inside a hot furnace. With an unwavering faith in his heart and a love for his Guru which could not be shattered, he prayed for a while and then calmly stepped into the furnace. At the same moment, his master, Guru Hargobind Singh Ji, miles away from him, asked his devotees to start pouring cold water over his body. The Sikhs (Devotees) obeyed his order and then wished to know the mystery behind all this. "Bhai Biddi Chand will come and tell you", was all the Guru said. Bhai Biddi Chand escaped unharmed. That is the level of the bond which exists between the Guru and his disciples. That is how far Guru Kripa can go.

In a way, each and every difficulty in life is a kind of subtle fire which can consume our body and mind. At such times, it is the parental care as well as guidance of the Guru which protects and saves us. No one of us can claim to have conquered all the forces of life and no one of us is beyond the reach of the cold perfection of the laws of nature. We are surrounded by an ocean of uncertainty and our boat is too fragile for making boastful declarations or blowing the trumpets of egoistic pride. Without the care and protection of a parent, how safe and secure can a child be? The relationship between a true master and his devotee is not a casual friendship; it is a commitment that is expected to pass every possible test in life. Even physical death should not be able to damage the sanctity of this bond. No matter how harsh are his circumstances, the disciple is never left at the mercy of his predicament by his master. He escapes every fire unharmed.

"As a plant needs protection from so many things to grow into a full - fledged tree, so does a man in search of meaning need protection from the insanity of the world."

V – Listening

I have spent thousands and thousands of hours just listening to the enlightened ones, through their audio and video recordings and it has no doubt proved to be the most powerful supporting system for my vision and conviction. Their words have served the purpose of a compass in the steering of my incarnation. At times the insanity of the world invaded my truth so fiercely that I found myself questioning the practicality of the path I had chosen. I was compelled by the dilemmas I faced, to strike a balance between my way of looking at things and the perception of the world. I never fully succeeded, but the gap could now be managed. I learnt through some bitter lessons that truth cannot be shared with those who are not yet ready for it. But it left me feeling quite deserted, lonely and betrayed.

For the dark ignorance of mankind, the wisdom of the enlightened beings serves the purpose of a lamp. It illumines all the corners with the brilliance of absolute truth. I also needed that lamp to illumine the path in front of me so that I could continue on my journey without losing direction. My own intuition was not powerful enough to guide me through the paradoxes of life and my wisdom had not yet developed to a point where it was enough unto itself. In the presence and words of the ones who had made it, after struggling with the basic illusions and attachments, I found the map that could help me locate the treasure which was waiting for me to be discovered. No worldly man could have described the inner landscapes, the nature of the mind and the traps laid out for the soul. Only the one who had moved within could tell me the way it is.

I started with listening to classical music, especially Ustaad Nusrat Fateh Ali Khan, Ustaad Ghulam Ali, Shrimati Lata Mangeshkar and Shri Puran Chand Wadali. As a student of music, it was an essential part of my learning and one of my subtle diets. But over the years, as my listening became very deep, music composed by God was enough for me and I no longer felt the need for an audio player. The chirping of a bird, the sound of a cricket, the playful sounds of innocent kids, the music created by water flowing through a narrow passage and all the divine frequencies reaching my ear from so many different sources were enough to quench the musician in me and enrich the silence of my soul. As a listener I think I was graduating to be able to listen to the wise ones.

It was in the year 1998 that Wishwpreet, a friend of mine, introduced me to an audio recording of a sermon by Acharya Rajneesh, famously known as Osho. I instantly got hooked to the intoxication of his truthful deliverance, poetic flavor and tons of intelligent humor, never out of alignment with the topic concerned. This, I think was my formal initiation into the strange world of the enlightened beings. The strong tone of truth in his talks pulled me out of all inhibitions and encouraged me to face myself for the first time in this incarnation. I could not hide behind my rationalizations anymore and I could not afford to postpone the transformation of my being. The essential message in his talks was clear - to liberate ourselves from the various visible and invisible imprisonments, as soon as possible.

When you listen to the one who knows, there is nowhere you can hide. Truth disarms you by robbing you of all your rationalizations. It does not let you escape from responsibility with clever justifications. It wakes you up to the fact that for every clever escape there is a price to be paid. It forces you to be prepared for the consequences of your actions in the past and act like a reasonable being in the present as well as the future. It launches direct attacks on the ego and defeats it like it has been never defeated before. It destroys every false belief and spares only that which is absolute. Just as the impurities in gold get burnt when it is passed through the flames of fire, the flames of truth reduce to ashes the cunning intelligence of man. But this liberates the soul from the exploitation of the mind.

To fall in love with the voice of the wise is to fall in love with God. To become comfortable with your vulnerability in the presence of wisdom and truth is the prerequisite for deserving the bliss that surpasses all understanding. Most of us are conditioned in a way to live a life of misery. The job of the wise ones is to heal our sick conditioning and introduce us to our own glory through methods that suit our basic nature. Over the years, I have developed such a taste for the peculiarity of every realized being that most of my need for companionship gets fulfilled simply by listening to them. Every sermon of theirs makes me move by an inch or two in the direction of my liberty. Every sermon reminds me of an area of my life which needs my attention or an attachment that needs to be renounced.

The effectiveness of listening as a meditation technique comes from the moments of thoughtlessness it can create through the deepening of your silence. There are moments when the activity of the mind is reduced to zero and you unknowingly slide into the dimension of pure awareness. Though you are able to stay there only for a short while and are pulled back into the thinking mind by some kind of thought or the other, but even this brief stay proves to be of immense significance in liberating you of your identification with thought. Deep listening can be the shortest shortcut to move into the space of "No Mind" because there is absolutely nothing to do in the practicing of the method. As soon as you become an ear and move away from the noise of the internal dialogue, the existence starts whispering to you all its secrets one by one. Once you have fully recognized, the taste of pure consciousness, it becomes easier to work on the elements which are a cause of distraction within. Without the dimension of awareness, witnessing would not have been possible and without the cultivation of the witness, liberty was out of question. So it is all a movement from A to B, B to C and C to D. Listening introduces you to silence and silence introduces you to consciousness. Consciousness introduces you to the soul and the soul introduces you to the almighty.

Listening to the sermons of the wise ones provides our being with a lot of spiritual clarity. It helps us organize our vision and enriches our perception. A view of the bigger picture of life is not available to everyone. One in a billion happens to be blessed with such an altitude. Realized beings help us look at things from a rare and unique angle and expand our perception through the inclusion of dimensions of reality which they have come to know and experience. In the very act of listening to their words and the silence between the words, we are transported to an altitude from where the various phenomenon of life can be seen in the light of ultimate truth. A lot of our confusion, pain and suffering, gets eliminated by the mere correction of our view and we are able to live the same old life with a newly found attitude.

The only precaution to be taken in the spiritual practice of listening to the wisdom of others is that it should not be allowed to become an addiction or an escape from a real contact with life. Wisdom is not a substitute for karmic responsibility or action. It is to know the difference between right and wrong, stick to the right and stay away from the wrong. But wisdom does not imply doing nothing at all and adopting a passive attitude towards social obligations and personal responsibilities. There is a very fine line between true renunciation and an escape from the challenges of living with honor and if you are not conscious enough, the comfort zone can drag you into unrighteous rationalizations. When you start listening for the sake of listening; beware. Don't let your spiritual practice become an opium for the mind. When you realize that a method has become an excuse of your convenience, be honest and live up to the challenges of your incarnation by consciously stepping out of your comfort zone.

The sermon of an enlightened being is like a milestone; it can only direct us towards our destination, it cannot take us there. It can tell us what to do but it cannot do it for us. Ultimately, we achieve anything out of our own effort; our own karma. Psychological work cannot be a substitute for physical action though it has a very substantial role to play in the manifestation of things and in designing the blueprint of our life. A milestone should be taken as only that which it is - a milestone. Dare to travel or walk the distance that needs to be travelled. Make sure that you are not using spirituality as an escape from the harsh practicalities of life. Make sure that your ideology is not camaflouged escapism. Be strong in self analysis and move ahead in life by confronting all the difficulties. Be courageous.

"Listening introduces you to silence and silence introduces you to consciousness; consciousness introduces you to the soul and the soul introduces you to the almighty."

VI – Relationships

Most of the decisions I made and which had a great impact on the unfolding of my incarnation, were made by my heart and not the mind. Being a Taurus, I think by my very nature, I am strongly driven by my emotions. I trust my intuition more than I trust the rational mind and I consider it to be a more evolved element of our being, more capable of comprehending the wisdom of the cosmos. The mind may be good at calculating, computing and analyzing, but it does not have the capability to host something as divine as compassion. It cannot solve the mesmerizing and mysterious equations of love. To deal with things like love and compassion you need a human heart, a heart that has not been corrupted by the clever manipulations of the thinking mind.

Relationships, owing to their high emotional content, have played a very major role in the sculpturing of my being and it took me quite a long time to realize that in order to become good at helping others, in attaining spiritual liberty, I had to master the art of relating; the art of using a relationship as a vehicle for mutual growth. The very nature of the kind of work I wish to do as a human being, requires that I do not let my personal preferences become a hindrance to my utility as an instrument of spiritual freedom. I am required to feel comfortable in the company of souls with unique ways of living their lives and relating with the presence or concept of God. The wisdom of Shri Ram Dass, formerly named Dr. Richard Alpert proved to be the most helpful to me, in explaining to myself, the intricacies of what he calls, "The Yoga of Relationships."

I remember all the instances, when I handled very unwisely, the emotional storms in my personal life born out of a difference in attitudes. They clearly swept me of my feet and rendered my wisdom, absolutely useless. Instead of being able to bring peace to those situations, I was adding my own anger and violence to them and thus becoming a part of the problem, rather than the solution. I could not stay a witness to the unfolding of my incarnation or the karmic give and takes and was overpowered by the energies that were threatening my sense of righteousness. I found myself failing to define Dharma through my actions and experienced the whole issue of relating, either as an emotional pain and helplessness or as a complexity beyond my grasp.

I was basically unable to maintain an adequate gap between myself and others and allowed the winds of ignorance to blow away the lamp of my consciousness. The linear flow of events completely captured my attention and the vertical dimension of life got ignored as a possibility. The space from where everything can be allowed to be the way it is, had not yet fully developed and I found myself desperately trying to rescue everyone, from the outcome of reckless behavior. Relationships can no doubt, prove to be the toughest aspect of a human incarnation because of the variables involved in the interaction between individuals. Thousands of incarnations can be responsible for the way the coming together of two souls unfolds and if you fall into the trap of appearances, it can sometimes be terribly heavy for the mind to make any sense out of it.

To be able to use relationships as a method for coming to God, you have to be firmly rooted in the dimension of awareness, so that, even when you are actively participating in the sophisticated dance of forms, there is a part of you looking at it all from a higher altitude. The art of relating successfully is all about not losing the divine perspective i.e. looking at the emotional ups and downs with the indifference of the witness. A space in your being has to be always available for the interaction of personalities and the merging or clashing of individual boundaries; a space which does not get occupied by the difference of opinion and allows for a non judgmental expression of the self. If people feel being analyzed and judged in your presence, then you have not yet cultivated the space I am talking about and need to work on yourself as an environment for growth.

The karmic package which each individual soul brings with itself, as the curriculum for its current incarnation can be so unique and peculiar that if you try to relate with anyone according to some rigid model of life, you will soon experience the lack of mutual understanding. Now, the problem is not with the person concerned; the problem is with your locked approach to the mystery you are surrounded by or come across. Everyone has his or her own way of living up to the challenges in life and deriving happiness from the innumerable experiences and phenomenon available. It all depends upon the variables involved in the unfolding of an incarnation. But when we start expecting the whole of mankind to look at the existence the way we do, we are really asking for it.

In case we have succeeded in liberating ourselves, the best we can do to assist someone, in the process of spiritual transformation, is to be available in a very non-violent way, as an instrument of knowing. We must not impose our wisdom on the expression of someone's uniqueness. The beauty of a relationship comes from the experience of oneness and that experience can only be invited by including the other and expanding. If the nature of our core temperaments allows for such a merging to be possible we should consider ourselves very fortunate but if a relationship lacks such a high level of intimacy, there should not be an overlapping or clashing of personalities. The other should be allowed to take his or her teachings from wherever he or she feels like and in a way which harmonizes with the state of the being.

If we could learn the art of just being with people, with no expectations regarding the outcome of our interactions, our personal world would be much healthier in terms of emotional balance. The energy of conversations and dialogues can be used to heal our emotional blocks by the enveloping of our interactions with a cloud of compassion. Why do you think we become capable of loving and forgiving in the presence of a Saint? Because the compassion of his heart converts our anger and hatred into love. He may not have asked us to love; he may not have asked us to forgive. But we feel being capable of doing so anyway. That's the power of true compassion - it transforms without even trying to transform. It heals without making an effort to do so. Our basic nature should be generous enough to allow everyone a healthy expression of his or her freedom.

There is absolutely no doubt about the fact that the most meaningful relationships in your life are going to be the ones that have got loyalty in them. And they will be very few. What about the rest? What about the ones that are not transparent enough for mutual trust to manifest? What about the ones which seem to distract you from the purpose of your incarnation? What about the ones which force you into a compromising stance? Will you allow them to become a burden for the soul and drag it into the dungeon of negativity? Will you allow them to inflict you with bitterness and sarcasm? You can avoid this spiritual corrosion by learning to allow each and every soul to flow in the direction of its decided course. You can liberate yourself from a lot of pain by living parallel to the world.

The utility of relationships as a vehicle for spiritual growth comes from the way they work, like what Shri Ram Dass calls, a sand paper, in the process of smoothing the rough edges of our being. Each and every interaction of ours with another human being has got something to teach. Each and every conversation of ours is a chance to explore another dimension of the life we live every day. Every soul looks at the existence from a different and unique angle. So much so that there are as many ways of living in this existence as there are souls in this cosmos. When two clouds of consciousness, two bodies and two intellects, play with each other through language, thought and emotions, a third possibility in the form of shared awareness comes into being which could not have manifested without an interaction. This shared awareness can help us grow and expand if we do not cling to any particular expectation from the outcome of our interactions. It can introduce us to subtle liberating experiences if we simply allow our interactions to flow at a natural pace and in the direction of compassion.

Strangely though, it is the difficult and impossible people in our life who make us grow the most and this happens against our will. They compel us to revise our perception regarding everything in life and make us give a serious thought to the meaning and purpose of our incarnation. But more often than not, it's a painful growth. This pain however can be reduced by consciously adopting a generous approach towards the nature of our karmic unfolding and the general layout of our incarnation. By developing a powerful witness, we can save ourselves from being carried away by the emotional cyclones of our life. The suffering which is sponsored by the spiritual gaps in our relationships can be transmuted into wisdom through the art of allowing and accepting. We can let the sand papers of ignorance and arrogance smooth and polish our ego.

Basically, all the relationships are a dance between oneness and duality and the quality of experience that any particular relationship has to offer, depends upon the amount of these two paradoxical dimensions in it. The more your interactions with a person push you into a defensive mode and remind you of your separation, the less fulfilling the relationship is. The more a relationship introduces you to the mysterious dimensions of love, the more blissful it is. In true love, one soul seems to have split into two complementary souls in order to experience the transformation of one into two and then back into one. But true love is rare. Nevertheless, we can use the interactions which pull us into separation as a spiritual practice for personal growth by consciously witnessing the dance between oneness and duality. The energy imprisoned by the ego can be released through a conscious distancing from it and by becoming available to the experience of the formless behind all forms.

"You can liberate yourself from a lot of pain by living parallel to the world."

VII – Breathing

If I were to suggest, a meditation technique to someone who has just begun his or her spiritual quest and is not much convinced by the reciting of a Mantra, it would be mindful breathing. Though most of us are inclined to underestimate its potential because of its simplicity, watching the breath can prove to be the most effective way of separating ourselves from our identification with the body, mind and senses. Like listening, it is one of the shortest shortcuts for sliding into the dimension of the witness; the "Sakshi". The moment you start watching the breath, the witness comes into being in its completeness and the confusion owing to the blending together of the various elements that go into the making of what you are, starts settling down like a precipitate. A few inhales and exhales can pull you out of your deepest illusions regarding the "Absoluteness" of your being.

It was a result of the efforts made by Swami Ramdev, through the various available means, for propagating the physical, psychological and spiritual benefits of Yoga, that I first got attracted to Pranayam - the formal practice of controlling the breath. I practiced only the six basic exercises which were Bhastrika Pranayam, Kapal Bhati Pranayam, Anulom Vilom Pranayam, Ujjayi Pranayam, Bhramri Pranayam and Sheetali Pranayam . But it was more than enough to begin with. The first time I looked at my watch to find out how long I could hold my breath or tried to stop myself from inhaling after a complete and deep exhale, I realized how fragile and vulnerable, was the invisible thread of life. I had felt the same way when I went under water during my initiation into swimming but Pranayam offered a total control over the comprehension of my experience.

It's easy to watch the breath as compared to watching an anger, lust or greed because the object of your observation can be felt by the nostrils. Its' form is much more solid than that of the subtle elements. With slight focusing of your awareness, you can tell whether you are inhaling and exhaling from the left nostril or right nostril or both of them. In case of things like anger and lust, such precise monitoring takes decades to master. In the act of witnessing your automatic breathing you get to know the taste of consciousness and once you have become acquainted with this taste you can move in and out of it as frequently as you wish to. You now know exactly what to achieve and you also know how to. With every passing day, you become better at playing with the fundamental components of your being. The breath becomes a ticket for you to travel outside the realm of thought and helps you identify with the one within that can watch the body breathing. It liberates your awareness from the captivity of mortality.

Now, if I am angry and I hold my breath, the anger won't be able to maintain itself. Without a continuous supply of "Pran" or life force in the form of the breath, it will come to a halt like an automobile having run out of fuel. Breath is what makes the transportation of thoughts and emotions possible between the mind and our Kleshas. The mind stops functioning in the absence of normal breathing and the connectivity of our invisible elements gets disrupted when we start exercising control over the inhale and exhale of breath. As soon as the various elements are separated, our awareness becomes available to us and can now be established in itself. This is what liberates it from the clutches of the body, mind and senses and makes it possible for us to move towards our soul, our actual self.

If you just watch your breathing and don't interfere with it at all, there comes a moment when the body is breathing automatically and you are standing at a distance. The experience of this passive stance can wake you up to all the wasteful expenditures of your precious spiritual energy. You realize that there is a lot in your life which does not need to be pushed and pulled and can work much more effectively without your deliberate effort. At times you would feel as if your body is a statue connected with the cosmos through the breath and you are someone residing in this statue like someone living in a rented house. These insights, though like a flash of lightening, will be very powerful in effect and will gradually separate you from your body the way the pulp of a coconut is separated from the shell.

The greatest benefit of using breath as a meditation technique is that like the Mantra, it is always readily available. You could be travelling in a bus or train, with nothing else to do, looking outside the window at the vast countryside. By just focusing on your breath, you can convert a boring and monotonous journey into an incredible inner experience. This simple technique of just watching the breath is known to have been responsible for the enlightenment of more beings on this planet than any other. It is called Vipassana meditation, which literally means – "To see things as they really are." The major difference between Vipassana and Pranayam is that in Pranayam we interfere with the natural pattern of breathing whereas in Vipassana, we just observe it. You will soon discover that the duration of exhale is 1 and a ½ or 2 times that of the inhale and between the inhale and exhale there is a gap which has got the potential to introduce us to the vertical dimension of our being.

If we speak in medical terms, then the job of breathing is to provide the body with oxygen and to help it get rid of carbon dioxide. That means, with a deep inhale, we can nourish every cell of the body with ample amount of life and with a deep exhale, we can empty ourselves of a lot of the cellular waste. It's a totally logical way of looking at the breath. However, when we practice Vipassana, our breathing assumes a significance which cannot be explained in scientific terms. The breath that most of us take for granted and don't even notice for months together, emerges to be the bridge which exists between the body and the soul. If you take it away, the two fall apart. If you refuse to take another breath, the soul will have no option but to separate from the body.

To be able to observe our breath like a spectator should be considered as a golden opportunity for liberating ourselves from our attachment to the body, mind and senses. Animals cannot breathe mindfully. Animals cannot meditate. Hence they cannot separate the basic elements we are all composed of. Man is supreme owing to his ability to step out of the wheel of birth and death. Awareness, as a dimension, is a blessing for the whole of mankind. The one who can observe the breath can also observe the internal dialogue of the mind and the seduction of the mind by the senses. All witnessing is done from the same one dimension - the consciousness and no matter which technique you practice for living a conscious life, it all boils down to the cultivation of this dimension. With our own breath as the object of our meditation, we can take a quantum leap in the direction of discovering who we really are.

"With our own breath as the object of our meditation, we can take a quantum leap in the direction of discovering who we really are."

VIII – Music

As kids, what fascinated me and my elder brother the most was movies, owing to their rich musical content and the ability to shift our minds into an altered state through flights of imagination. These were the years that followed 1975. I was three years old by then and could appreciate a piece of good music, in my own way. Coincidently, this was the decade, when the greatest musicians of the twentieth century had come together, under the banner of the film industry in Bombay. Songs that had the power to make you bloom like a lotus or cry were being composed and sung by a team of artists who lived for the sake of expressing themselves through words, notes and beats. Though, as a child, I could not interpret the lyrics, but my soul was anyway nourished by the melodies that floated around in the ethers. Music obviously had a lot to do with my previous incarnations.

It was in the year 1995, when I became a student of classical music and started taking formal training, that music as a spiritual practice started occupying a major part of my daily routine. The writing down of music on paper in the form of notation proved to be a very big change in the way I related with all kinds of sounds. The division of the dimension of time into fixed intervals in the form of patterns of rhythm was something I had never even thought about. The melodies that so far used to be just a pleasure of the senses for me, changed into beautiful paintings made on the canvas of silence by dipping the brush in notes and beats. The various "Raags" created through the permutation and combination of all the different frequencies and their potential to impress or express an emotion introduced my being, in a very seductive way, to the subtle world of vibrations.

It was absolutely natural for me to have got attracted to the field of music because I was born with a voice that was good enough to be a successful playback singer in the music industry. Music was for me, what water is for the fish or what sky is for a bird. We were made for each other. But once I formally got admitted to an institute as a regular student, it was destined to become my way of living for the next two decades. Now, when you try to convert your passion into a profession, there is a very big shift that takes place in the way you look at pleasure and pain. The harsh practical details which surround the issue of our basic survival leave no space for empty talk and indulgence in lazy attitude. I reluctantly have to admit that I could not really succeed as a professional musician, most probably because of some big contradiction in my basic desire system. But I surely made huge spiritual gains that compensated for all my struggles as an artist and my sense of failure as a professional.

My daily practice of the "Raags" which is known as "Riaz" in the world of Indian classical music, introduced me to the transmutation of energy by converting me into a musical instrument with the help of my vocal chords. Music took me far beyond the body and laid down a very strong foundation for some serious spiritual work that I was required to do as an ascetic. Mesmeric performances by legendary artists like Ustaad Nusrat Fateh Ali Khan provided me with the experience of dimensions quite close to bliss. But by the year 2013, my responsibilities as a father, husband, brother, son, citizen and human being compelled me to seriously think about how to earn a living and say good bye to everything which could not feed my family. And that got me into real estate.

Having bought and sold about a dozen plots of land and a 200 sq. ft. shop in a market, the revolutionary in me started looking for a way to express itself and make a contribution in steering the world towards self-realization. Music could not do that since the imprisonment of the self is too complex to be fully addressed in a song, even if it were devotional. This led me to writing about, all that I knew regarding the nature of this existence and I am completely satisfied, with the ability of written word to assist someone in moving from point A to point B on the path of salvation. What I am doing as an author, I could not never have done as a professional musician. It seems that all my setbacks and failures in the past were nothing but blessings in disguise. I think when you are moving in the right direction and your destination is certain, it really does not matter what route you take.

Today, when I listen to a piece of good music I listen from a space totally different from the one I used to twenty years ago. I feel as if I am residing in a dimension where even the greatest of symphonies cannot take you. It's a state of being where most of the worldly music sounds like a noise or disturbance and an overuse of any of the senses becomes a fatigue after some time. Resting in a silence which is beyond the chattering of the mind and the violence of temptations I can look back at the role each and every vehicle of transformation played in landing me here. Music surely was very instrumental in helping me evolve and in the transition from a three dimensional reality to the mysterious wisdom of the cosmos. But now that I have exploited it enough for all the potential it has got, I find the parent silence of the existence much more promising and blissful.

As a technique for cultivating your consciousness, I think music is used most intensively by the ones who mix and master music tracks. I have done a bit of it myself and I know how deep you have to dive into the world of sound and rhythm for bringing out a track well mixed. There comes a point when you can notice the difference that a fraction of note or beat can make. Like a pencil sharpened by a sharpener, your sense of hearing is sharpened to such an extent that it can almost hear the inaudible. The balancing of left and right channels, the panning of sounds and the decibel count can demand such a deep involvement that you will find your consciousness being drifted into unknown realms and experiences.

The beauty of using music as a spiritual practice lies in the fact that there is an immediate payoff which is as satisfying as its long term benefits. Every hour of a religious practice leaves you relaxed, enriched and attuned. There is a daily increment in your awareness of the subtle dimensions and a movement in the direction of salvation. Working on invisibles such as sound and rhythm starts with a detachment from the body and all those senses which are not required to move into the depths of the task at hand. It is therefore a kind of partial renunciation because other than the mind and your sense of hearing, there is very little else involved. From the spring board of this state of being, an occasional leap into pure consciousness can be easily made through practice.

"I think when you are moving in the right direction and your destination is certain, it really does not matter what route you take."

IX – Food

If an ordinary man is left alone, his routine soon starts revolving around food, sleep and the sexual drive, without his being aware of it. To a large extent, even the extraordinary are affected by the primordial stuff built into our species. The words, "Man is a social animal", point towards our basic instincts that cannot be mastered or conquered, by lukewarm or half hearted attempts. Food is an aspect of our life that needs to be disciplined the most if we aspire to achieve anything significant in the realm of spiritual freedom. The nature of the mind, both conscious and sub-conscious, exhibits in the form of habits, most strongly and obviously in the case of food. So if you wish to tame your mind, the best way to do that is by exercising control over your eating habits.

The first time I became aware of the part which food plays in determining our health, was when I suffered from a severe chest infection and had to go for a one month restricted diet, as advised by a naturopath. The only three things I could take were milk, fruits and fruit juice. Since it was summer, I usually opted for mangoes. Those four weeks of partial fasting introduced me to the medicinal value of natural foods and also the amount of discipline required to follow a strict diet regimen. It was the first time I encountered the extreme in my eating habits in all its absolute fierceness. I realized how much I had taken for granted the functioning of the various organs in my body and how little respect as well as concern I had practiced with regards to the temple in which I lived. By the end of my natural therapy, my relationship with food had completely been revised and it dawned on me that we must not eat or drink anything just for the sake of pleasure.

For quite a few years after my sickness, I frequently used to fast for a day or two to cleanse my body of all its toxic wastes and it was because of the lack of physical strength during a complete fast that I became highly conscious of my energy body. When you have had no solid diet for two or three days, even something as simple as getting up from a chair or having to stand for a while feels like a laborious act. I noticed that there was something other than my physical body which determined my sense of well being. This awareness became my initiation into the subtle world of thoughts, emotions, senses and consciousness.

I came across an interesting line in one of the books on naturopathy, "Eat the liquids and drink the solids", which literally means, you should chew the solid foods so well that they take a liquid form and you should drink the liquids so meditatively as if you are eating them. I started practicing this and very soon, food became a very effective method for me to move within. My sense of taste was converted into waves of pleasure, which could take me beyond the mind, if surfed consciously. I learnt how to slide from the "Experiencer" into the experience itself and use my taste buds to introduce me to that which cannot be tasted with the senses. As a result of all this practice, the quantity of my meals got reduced and the quality of my eating got improved.

You may not have ever given it a thought that we don't only eat when we are hungry; we eat when we are sad and depressed, we eat when we are lonely, we eat when we are rejected, we eat when we feel defeated, we eat when we are overwhelmed by the meaninglessness of events which are beyond the grasp of our understanding. There is a child in us that clings to the mother's breast every time it feels insecure. We use food, sleep, sex and drugs to escape from the pain of a reality that seems too intense to be perceived as a process of awakening. We use food as an addiction and not as nourishment for the body, mind and soul. I still sometimes catch myself doing that, though less frequently, so strong is our basic attraction towards all the edible stuff.

Sitting cross-legged on the floor, with a comfortable carpet beneath and our meal in front of us, when we meditatively eat and drink with the realization that ultimately it is Brahma i.e. us, offering Brahma i.e. food to Brahma i.e. the hunger, every meal becomes a way to worship the almighty. With such a respect for food, when you take up the responsibility of feeding your body, the taste buds cannot distract you from the divine purpose of eating. The four senses of smell, sight, taste and touch, actively involved in the nourishing of our body with foods and drinks, when used wisely, can help us cultivate a dimension which can exercise control over all the various elements of our being. Awareness gained through meditative eating can be extended to all those aspects of our life that have suffered at the hands of a spiritual slumber. Food can prove to be a great vehicle for moving towards the self.

Decades ago, a very remarkable experiment was carried out by some of the best naturopaths in the world. They took a bunch of kids, suffering from various minor ailments and left them alone in a hall with all kinds of fruits, vegetables and healthy drinks, laid out on a dining table. When each of the kids felt hungry, he or she picked up a fruit, vegetable or drink that was actually a medicine for his or her particular ailment. This certified the fact that they were being guided by a dimension which was far beyond the reach of the medical profession. We can call it intuition; we can call it consciousness. This dimension can be used to decide what to eat or drink and what not to and thus convert every meal of ours, into a source of healing. If you could establish a communion with your intuition and meditate for a few minutes before every meal, you would find yourself in a much better position to decide what is good for you.

Food not only becomes our flesh, bones, blood and semen, it also becomes our thought. Just notice how much the content of your dreams has to do with what you have for supper. From blissful conversations with a divine entity to nightmares of hostility, violence, suffering and loss, there is a wide range of experiences available to the soul and the subconscious mind, while we are sleeping and to a great extent, it is affected by the quality and quantity of our meal. Even when we are awake, the nature of our thought patterns is decided to a great degree, by the nature of our food intake. It is for this reason that every real Saint emphasizes on the giving up of non-vegetarianism. A pure, natural diet is guaranteed to play a significant role in cultivating pure and natural thoughts though you may have to complement it with other spiritual practices that support your core desire.

Now, the challenge involved in using food as a method for becoming more aware lies in rising above indulgence. The pleasure one derives from eating or drinking must not be allowed to defeat the very purpose of the act. The senses must not be offered the reigns of our body, mind and consciousness. Everything should be put, where it belongs. Our kitchen and our refrigerator should be a source of health, energy and vitality not indulgence, sickness and addictions. We should not allow our sensual gratifications to dig our graves for us; we should tame all the wild desires that can take us away from our essential purpose. Food is supposed to help us perform all our duties in a graceful way and provide us with the zest required to move in the direction of our goal, whether material or spiritual. You need food to win a gold medal in the Olympics, you need it to invite material abundance in your life, it is required to fight all kinds of battles, it is required to meditate and reach out to God; there is nothing worthwhile that can be achieved without the support of an adequate diet. Food is worth worshiping and the ideal way to do that is by eating and drinking sensibly.

"Food is supposed to help us perform all our duties in a graceful way and provide us with the zest required to move in the direction of our goal, whether material or spiritual."

The River Of Life

Riding on our temperaments, it takes its decided course,
The "River of Life" flows through us, replacing the old with new.

Nothing can question its pace or direction, no one can change its mind,
If you go with the flow, it makes you wise; if you don't, it allows you to
tire.

At times it is calm, at times it is wild; the pattern of these tides is strange,
With all the compassion in your heart there can be, you still could be going
to war.

The change is so constant, the flux so impeccable, the current so convinced
and so strong,
If you try to resist you are lifted off your feet and simply swept along.

The day and the night, the seasons of the year, the cycle of birth and death,
With all these wheels it keeps on moving, without a moment of rest.

People keep walking in and out of your life, your heart keeps on looking
for more,
Enduring all the pain, it falls in love again, for something that is sure.

Flowing through the eras, centuries and decades, it never runs out of its
force,
The laws with which it creates its path are beyond the grasp of a mind.

Prepared to go wherever it takes I am trying to know all I can about its
flow,
I do not want to die like a fool, I wish to realize and grow.

This river of life flowing through me, could take me back to my home,
Where I could rest in peace, desire no more and feel as light as foam.

I trust these waves that play with my soul, pushing it towards the bank,
I finally recognize the Grace of God in all its vigorous disguises.

••••••••••••••••••••••••••••••••••

ABOUT THE AUTHOR

Shri Charanjit Singh was born in the Patiala district of Punjab, in village Dhenthal, on the 30th of April 1972. His father, Shri Kulwant Singh, served as a senior auditor in the cooperative bank and his mother Swarn Kaur was a simple housewife. Shri Saudagar Singh, the author's grandfather, was a hard core meditator and a man of Truth and it was most probably, his occasional company in the initial years that introduced the author's soul to the taste of Bhakti or devotion. In 1972, Shri Kulwant Singh got transferred to the Sangrur district and so the whole family shifted to this town. Along with his elder brother Manjit Singh, who later joined the Indian Army and is now serving as a P.C.S. officer, this kid studied from nursery to the fifth standard in General Gurnam Singh Public School Sangrur. In 1979, this family was blessed with another baby boy Harjit Singh who is now an upcoming pop star living in Sydney; Australia. The author has some beautiful memories of this first decade of his incarnation and the word Sangrur means to him a lot more than just the name of another town. In 1983 Shri kulwant Singh got posted back to Patiala and the younger two kids got admitted in Yadavindra Public School Patiala (Y.P.S.) Elder brother Manjit went to Sainik School Kapurthala and from there to N.D.A. and I.M.A. From the sixth to the twelvth standard, Shri Charanjit Singh studied here. The family started living at the village which was approximately 22 Kilometers from school and stayed here for the next 19 years.

These were the years when the province of Punjab was going through a very violent change. The environment of the village was also not healthy for a soul as sensitive as that of the author. Both these factors had a very profound effect on the consciousness of this young boy and his inner world went through a metamorphosis. This was his initiation into the quest for meaning and though after passing out from the school in 1990, he became an engineering student, but the inner turmoil did not let him concentrate on his studies and after quitting in the third year of his degree, he started taking formal training in classical as well as western music from two different institutes in Pune. Music provided his aimless life with a meaning and a purpose and it also took care of his spiritual restlessness. The notes and beats made more sense than the assignments back in the engineering college.

During the transition from, saying goodbye to a full-fledged career in engineering, to pursuing his passion of music, Shri Charanjit Singh came in contact with the spiritual mentor of the Namdhari sect of Sikhs, Satguru Jagjit Singh Ji and he firmly believes that this power is protecting and guiding him even today. Shri Charanjit Singh has no doubt regarding the difference that Guru Kripa makes in the life of a Shishya, a disciple. From his own experience, he knows that all which is praiseworthy in him and his personal world, is not just a result of his own efforts; much of it is his Guru's blessings.

Along with music, Shri Charanjit Singh became deeply interested in the various meditation techniques, especially the ones designed by Acharya Rajneesh and being practiced at the Ashram in Koregaon Park Pune. The potential of these techniques, in liberating an individual from the prison of the mind and the suffering it creates, held great promise for this young revolutionary who was looking for ways to deal with the pain that is inherent in a human incarnation. With the purification of his soul and the evolution of his consciousness, Shri Charanjit Singh became increasingly aware of the part or role he played in the unfolding of life and also his responsibility as a conscious being, with regard to the degradation of human values and corruption of all kinds on such a large scale, in the environment, of which, he was an integral part. He realized that the glory of wisdom is in it being able to serve humanity by illuminating the lives of fellow beings with compassion and consciousness. This book is also an expression of his concern for the whole of mankind and the realization of his own duty. Through words, he is encouraging each and every one of us to establish religiousness inside and around us since that is the only way to keep this earth livable.

Any religious person has got basically three means to share his vision, his perception with the rest - books, audio/video recordings and personal contact. There was an era when personal contact was the only option available. All the three modes have got their benefits and limitations. For example, the way you can go into the details and intricacies of an issue in a book, is not possible in a chance conversation. But the shared awareness that comes into being in a conversation and the resonance of vibrations that manifests through a personal meeting of compatible souls, cannot be expected from the reading of a book or the listening of an audio recording. Shri Charanjit Singh is also making an honest attempt in using the mediums available to him to reach out to sincere souls like you. If a welfare organization feels the need of the service he has to offer, he tries his best to live up to their expectations. Wherever he is felt needed, he gives 1-2 hr. talks on the topics of Dharma, Karma, Guru Kripa, addiction, spiritual freedom and meditation. In every possible way, he tries to help as well as serve the rest of us, knowing very well his limitations and capacity as a human being.

Moksh Publications

www.ingramcontent.com/pod-product-compliance
Lightning Source LLC
Chambersburg PA
CBHW021130020426
42331CB00005B/700